INTRODUCTION

"When that careers officer asks what you want to do, and you say you want to be a spacewoman, and they say, 'Now, what do you really want to do?', tell them to * * * * off!"

Geri Halliwell, singer

Here's two words guaranteed to send you diving for cover under your duvet – 'jobs' and 'careers'! They don't just get us panicking about exam results and qualifications. They also make us think of fusty careers 'advisors', offering highly useful 'advice', like if you only paid as much attention to your work as you did to gossiping at the back of the class, then you might eventually manage to become a secretary. Well, don't let them fob you off. Certainly listen to their advice, but make sure they listen to your dreams, too.

This book is designed to help you find your dream job. It's divided into cunningly handy sections, so once you've found out more about yourself in the first one, you'll be able to jump straight to the bit which interests you (where the jobs are!). There are also heaps of contact details for professional organisations who'll be able to offer further help. Although many of these are based in London, you can call them – or visit their websites – for sister companies elsewhere in the UK.

Careers? You really can do it! And your future's literally in your hands.

KEY TO QUALIFICATIONS
showing equivalence of academic and
vocational (i.e. job-related) qualifications

Level 5 Degree
NVQ5: National Vocational Qualification. Mostly
gained in the workplace as they're job-specific

Level 4 Part degree
BTEC HNC/HND: Business Technology &
Education Council Higher National
Certificate/Diploma
GNVQ4: General National Vocational
Qualification. Mostly studied at school or
college. See page 8
NVQ4

Level 3 A level: Advanced level
BTEC National Certificate/Diploma:Equals 2 or
more A levels
Advanced GNVQ: Equals 2 or more A levels
NVQ3

Level 2 GCSE (Grades A–C): General Certificate of
Secondary Education
BTEC First Certificate/Diploma: Equals 2 or
more GCSEs (A–C)
Intermediate GNVQ: Equals 2 or more GCSEs
(A–C)
NVQ2

Level 1 GCSE (Grades D–G)
Foundation GNVQ: Equals 2 or more GCSEs
(D–G)
NVQ1

IMPORTANT NOTE

1 To keep things simple, this book refers only to GCSEs and NVQs, instead of their Scottish equivalents, SCEs and SVQs – they're practically the same.

2 Advanced level GNVQs have recently been replaced by new-look 'vocational A levels'. Foundation and Intermediate level GNVQs will be replaced by new-look 'vocational GCSEs' from September 2002, in subjects likely to include catering, information technology, manufacturing, health care, engineering and art and design. No reference has therefore been made to any form of GNVQ in later sections of this book.

MONEY, MONEY, MONEY

Want to know what you'll earn? Each job includes a guide to salary, but remember that many organisations don't want to divulge exact figures. In other cases, there are so many different stages or levels within that job, that it's difficult to give an 'average' salary. The way in which each pay figure has been reached is clearly indicated in each case.

Chapter 1

WHO AM I?

"If you don't know what you want to do, don't worry as things take time to work themselves out."

Ant McPartlin, TV presenter

Who am I? You're probably already thinking that's a silly question. After all, you've been on this planet for over ten years, and if you didn't know who you are, you'd be in a hospital ward full of amnesiacs.

But although you know the stuff like your name and which boys are hot this month, that's not enough to help you choose a future career. The things that make up 'you' should have a lot of influence on the job you end up doing. Around 80 per cent of people lose their jobs, or leave them, at some time in their lives, because they don't fit in, so it definitely helps if you're suited to it in the first place! Find out more about yourself with this quick quiz:

QUIZ
What kind of person are you?

Finding out will help you find a career you'll enjoy.
How to play: Answer each question, ticking the one statement that most suits you. There's no right or wrong, and you should be as honest as you can.

1 What do you most enjoy doing at weekends?
a Meeting up with a big group.
b Going out with your best mate.
c Getting together with a few friends.
d Doing something on your own.

2 It's time for a class test. Do you:
a Look really enthusiastic – you love tests?
b Get a bit worried, but you know you'll get through it?
c Stress out – they're just not your strong point?
d Smile but inside you're a bit worried?

10

3 You're making your entrance at a house party, do you say:

a "Hey, I'm here! Who's got the video camera?"

b "Who wants a game of doubles on the Dreamcast?"

c "Where's the fruit punch? Can I get anyone a drink?"

d "I knew I should've got here earlier to set the place up."?

4 Which of these things do you like doing with your evening?

a Going bowling.

b Going to see a movie or a gig.

c Helping out with a local youth group.

d Watching TV.

5 It's a new term and there are big, awkward changes in your timetable. Do you feel:

a Pretty prepared – you guessed last week that things would probably be different?

b A bit annoyed – it's frustrating when things get changed around?

c Pretty agreeable – these things have to alter every so often?

d Sure you can suggest some ways of making it even better?

6 What do you most enjoy reading?
a Magazines like *Bliss*, *Smash Hits* or *Looks*.
b Regular fiction.
c Newspapers – anything from *The Daily Mail* to *The Times*.
d Sci-fi.

7 You've got heaps of homework, but Mum also asks you to help around the house and walk the dog, do you:
a Tackle each task one at a time, and get them all done with no hassle?
b Work out which will take you the least time, get that done first, then get on with everything else?
c Assure her it'll all be fine if you take a task at a time?
d Moan, then pay a friend to do your homework while you do the other stuff?

8 Which celeb do you admire the most?
a Carol Vorderman.
b Britney Spears.

c Richard Branson.

d Anita Roddick (founder of The Body Shop).

9 What would be your favourite kind of holiday?

a Something exciting that you've meticulously planned yourself, like trekking around Australia.

b Going somewhere that takes in all kinds of exotic locations – from Cuba to Thailand.

c Ibiza, with a big group of mates who are up for a laugh.

d Somewhere familiar that you've been to before with your mum or dad.

10 Take a look in your school bag. Is it:

a Neatly ordered, with all your folders and files labelled?

b A mess, but you can find everything in a flash?

c A complete joke – everything's mixed up?

d Quite messy, but that's how it's always been?

Scores

Work out your total score by matching the letters you chose with the numbers overleaf. Then write it in the box provided, as you'll be needing it later.

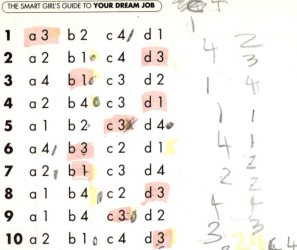

1 a 3   b 2   c 4   d 1
2 a 2   b 1   c 4   d 3
3 a 4   b 1   c 3   d 2
4 a 2   b 4   c 3   d 1
5 a 1   b 2   c 3   d 4
6 a 4   b 3   c 2   d 1
7 a 2   b 1   c 3   d 4
8 a 1   b 4   c 2   d 3
9 a 1   b 4   c 3   d 2
10 a 2   b 1   c 4   d 3

My **Who Am I?** score is . . .

Phew! You're now halfway to finding out all about yourself. Now go to Chapter Two . . .

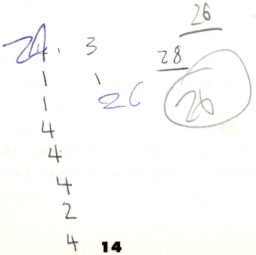

Chapter 2

YOUR JOB DREAMS

"Think about what you've always wanted to do — always, always wanted to do. Then try that, and work really hard. It's important to go for your dreams!"

Emma Bunton, Spice Girl

There's no point in finding out who you are, and what job you're suited to, if actually doing it would be more boring than a rainy fortnight in Clacton-on-Sea. Work can and should be fun, which is important when you realise you'll spend an average of 72,000 hours, or 9,000 days doing it over the next forty-something years. So you should aim towards your dream job in the first place.

Spend some time thinking about what you really, really want to do, and it will help you achieve your dreams. Be bold and think beyond that! Keep an open mind to anything!

On the other hand, don't stress out about this. In our grandparents' day, people had a job for life. These days, it's far easier to acquire new skills and change career paths several times during your working life.

If you've no idea about your dream job, the quiz that's coming up will help. (Then go to Chapter Three to discover the job type for you.)

WORK EXPERIENCE

The thought of work experience is a total nightmare. Who wants to be working for free when you can be out sunbathing/at the movies with your mates/ogling cute boys down the mall? Especially if it's something you're doing because your school says you must. But if you see work experience as a chance to try various jobs before you sign your life away, it's different. You'll make some useful contacts for the future, and see the different ways different people work. It'll also help your CV if you can show several periods of work experience related to your chosen career. So, try to get as much expe- rience as you can in all the areas you're interested in. Many of the people featured in the case studies in this book swear by their periods of work experience for helping them get where they are today.

So, what are you waiting for? Get out into the wonderful world of work, and feel what it's really like!

QUIZ

What's your dream job?

Chef or police officer, you'll cook up the answers and lay down the law . . .

How to play: Answer each question, 'picking up' each symbol next to the one answer that most suits you. Once again, there's no correct answer and honesty's vital!

1 Do you want a job that mostly uses your:

a Imagination? ●
b Brain power? ◆
c Love of people? ■
d Ability with numbers? ▲

2 What are your favourite school subjects?
a Community studies. ■
b Maths. ▲
c Sciences. ◆
d Drama. ●

2 What will be your attitude to your boss?
(Think about how you behave around teachers!)
a They'll wind me up when they tell me what to do. ◆

b I'll respect them, as they'll know what they're talking about. ▲

c I'll wish they'd just leave me to get on with things. ■

d Most times, I reckon I'll know better than them. ●

4 Would your working day:

a Start at 9 and end at 5.30 – you'd rather forget about work when you get home? ▲

b Start and finish at set times, but they'd vary? ■

c Always be a bit uncertain – who knows how many hours you'll work today? ●

d Consist of pretty long hours, but who cares when you love your job? ◆

5 Would you prefer to work:

a In various environments? ●

b Outdoors? ■

c In an office? ▲

d From home? ◆

6 Do you think you'll see other colleagues as:

a Sometimes useful, but it's good to do things on your own? ◆

19

b Pretty useful, although they'll sometimes get in the way? ▲

c Very helpful; it's great to work together for a common cause? ■

d Sometimes essential, sometimes completely unnecessary?! ●

7 Do you think you're mostly:

a Logical? ▲

b Creative? ●

c Analytical? ◆

d Persistent? ■

8 What's your attitude to GCSE coursework?

a You don't like presenting it, but you love the research. ◆

b You like deciding how it's all going to look. ●

c Getting stuck in is great, as long as everything is explained thoroughly. ■

d You like working through it methodically and get a buzz out of finishing. ▲

9 How important do you think it'll be to earn heaps of cash in your career?

a Vital – that's all you want from a job. ▲

b Not very important at all. ■

c Money would be nice, but you really want to love your job, too. ● ✓

d You've hardly even thought about it. ◆

10 Finally, do you want a job that:

a Fully stretches your talents? ◆ ✓

b Helps others? ■

c Brings you fame? ● ✓

d Keeps you on your toes? ▲

Scores

Now check which symbol you have the most of. Then write your score in the box overleaf, according to the following ratings:

If you have:

More ● than anything else: 40 points

More ■ than anything else: 30 points

More ▲ than anything else: 20 points

More ◆ than anything else: 10 points

21

IMPORTANT NOTE

If you have a matching number of symbols — say five squares and five circles — you should give yourself two separate scores. Then work your way through the book assuming the first score, then the other — it simply shows you're suited to a wider variety of careers.

My **Dream Job** score is . . .

Now comes the exciting bit. In Chapter Three you'll find out the type of job that suits you.

Chapter 3

JUST THE TYPE

"You could be an MP, the next Prime Minister, the next big scientist, a great artist!"

Geri Halliwell, singer

After all those cryptic questions, this chapter contains the moment of truth. It's time to discover which kind of job you're going to be best for, and enjoy the most. Add together your two scores from the quizzes in Chapters One and Two, and you'll find that you fit into one of four 'types' outlined below: **i** Creative & Media, **ii** Serving & Caring, **iii** Business & Finance or **iv** Science, IT & Engineering. Some of these won't mean much to you now, but they say heaps about your personality and abilities. Read on, and all will be revealed.

My **Who Am I?** score ☐ +

my **Dream Job** score ☐ = ☐

IMPORTANT NOTE

What if your final Dream Job score makes you fall somewhere near the edge of two of the four categories shown below? For example, you score 64, so you're teetering between Creative & Media and Serving & Caring. Well, don't worry. It could just be that you have some characteristics in each category and that you're suited to certain jobs in either field. So read about all the jobs in both of those sections to see what takes your fancy. Also, remember that although some characteristics will definitely apply to you, others won't – it is the general feel of the personality and job which is important.

40 +
28
——
68

24

Dream Job score = over 66. You're a . . .
Creative & Media type

You're got a great imagination, which means you're coming up with new ideas to showcase your talents, 24/7! People love you, not only because you're up on the latest showbiz gossip – from Dawson's Creek, to Richard Blackwood or the Backstreet Boys to All Saints – but because you've got excellent people skills. In fact, you're so outgoing you make Graham Norton look like a shrinking violet! Although organisation isn't your strong point, you're good in a small team and even happy to manage projects on your own.

You want a job where you'll do different things every day, juggling lots of problems and projects which use all your skills – if you just had one thing on the go, you'd soon get bored. You're certainly against being told what to do (although you like to learn). You'd prefer working in different places and you know your working hours will be varied, but that doesn't faze you. You're not looking for the highest paid job, although big bucks would be great if they came along!

You're ambitious, and will do anything to get to the top, even though you're happy to start at the very bottom. The job you take needs to have few rules, and even those can be broken! The main thing that will make you tick in your dream job is seeing your ideas become reality. Great, because the world's your stage!

The best

Your dream job: pop star, model, journalist, fashion designer, actor, chef, editor. Find out more about these, and more related careers, in the following chapters.

Dream Job score = 48–66. You're a . . . Serving & Caring type

You've got a smile that would challenge Ricky Martin in a Grin Of The Year Contest, and a personality to match. People love you, thanks to your patient attitude, your kindness and your ability to go out of your way for anyone or anything. You'd like a job where you can really make a difference to people's lives through 'hands-on' work – one where you can really get stuck in.

You'll work well in a team, as you love aiming for a common goal, but you're also good at coming up with ideas and implementing them on your own. You like to follow a chain of command, so you'll get on well with your boss. Even when you reach the top yourself, you'll always be friendly to others. You're happy facing new challenges, but you don't always look forward to change. And although you like set hours, you don't mind if that's doing shifts. Money's not at the top of your needs from a career, and you're pretty flexible about working indoors or outside. In fact, as long as you're working with people or animals and helping them, you'll be happy in whatever you do.

Your dream job: vet, teacher, retail manager, doctor, nurse, policewoman. Discover more about your dream job, and similar careers, in the following chapters.

Dream job score = 30–47. You're a . . . Business & Finance type

Every group of mates has a 'sensible' friend, and that's you. You're pretty much set in your ways, but that's no bad thing, if that's how you're comfortable. When it comes to doing things, it helps you sort your head out if everything's prearranged and decided. Even better if you've planned things carefully and methodically yourself – you like to be in control. Control's important when it comes to money too, but you have a rebellious streak.

You want a job where you'll work in a safe and stable environment, with a set career path to follow. It'll have to be one where you can use your brain, as you love solving problems. You thrive on pressure, and handle it well, because you're very organised. So you'll always know where you've put your favourite pen, or where you filed that important magazine.

You realise there's a lot to learn, so you're respectful of authority – especially if your work receives praise. Personally, you like to boss people around occasionally, and you'd rather that was a small group instead of a massive one.

You'd be happiest doing a normal working day, with the option of leaving your work behind at the office when 5.30 p.m. comes! And you'd prefer to work in the same place every day. Whether that's behind a desk or in a courtroom, you might not be that bothered yet – as long as you're using your brain!

Your dream job: lawyer, civil servant, accountant, stockbroker. There's more on these jobs, and others, in the following chapters.

Dream Job score = under 30. You're a...
Science, IT & Engineering type

Have you got a forehead like those blokes in the Tefal ads? If so, it's no surprise, as you've got a great brain, perfectly tuned to understand complex ideas that leave others completely confused. A right Carol Vorderman, you'll love a job where you can work through problems ("I'll have one from the top row, one from the next, and the rest from anywhere you choose please, Carol!"). In fact, you're always testing yourself and trying to overcome life's mysteries. You're always ahead of the latest trends and you love discovering new things – you probably mastered text messaging first, and use the internet more than many of your mates. And are all your CDs filed in alphabetical order? It's just that you're highly organised, and you like order and control in your life. So you would rather work in one place instead of moving around.

You'd like a career where you can work on your own, but you recognise the fun of having a group of mates around occasionally. Being bossy certainly isn't really your thing – and you don't like being told what to do – though you'll happily explain things to others . . . if they'll be able to understand you!

You'll probably have to work quite long hours in your future job, which is likely to be quite well paid – but the money and hours don't really bother you. Really, as long as you're challenged and you can use your mathematical brain, you'll be happy.

Your dream job: computer programmer, web designer, engineer, scientist, researcher. Look into these jobs and others in the following chapters.

Now you know your type, you're ready to find out more about your career options in Section Two. Well, nearly . . .

Chapter 4

Q & A
JOB DILEMMAS

Not all the problem letters we receive at *Bliss* magazine are about periods, boys, boobs or friendship traumas. Quite often, people are stressing about their future, with letters like these, sent to our Job Doctor . . .

Me, myself and I

I've heard it's important to find out who I am before I decide on a future career. That's ridiculous. I'm Tammy Jones, I'm 16, and I come from Liverpool. What else could I possibly need to know?

When you get a job, it's something you're going to be doing for a long time. So it's important to make sure you've made the right choice, or you'll spend ages being either **a** extremely unhappy or **b** moving from job to job, trying to find something you enjoy. Try to work out what you'll enjoy from the start, which you can do by looking at what you're into and thinking carefully about that. You can do a personality test; these exist on a number of careers websites, and will tell you more about who you are and also your job dreams.

It's also a good idea to ask other people how they see you, as you're not always going to be the best judge of that yourself. That's particularly true if you haven't done that well at school. Do all this, and you stand a far better chance of starting your working life in a happy, stress-free way. And keeping it like that.

Stalker talker
Everyone's always going on about work experience, but what's the best way of trying to get some? Nobody's going to want me shadowing them for a week, getting in their way.

Chances are, your school will send you on compulsory work experience in Year 10 or 11, so you'll get advice then on how to apply. It's easy to see this as an excuse for two weeks off, but you'll find it far more useful if you use the time to find out more about a job you think you'll be interested in and see it as a trial run.

If you want to apply for work experience, just send your CV and a covering letter to the Personnel Department of several companies you'd be interested in working at (don't just rely on one!). Flattery gets you everywhere, so explain why you'd like to work at their office (you've always read their mag/admired their work/ thought they're brilliant and you'd be a fantastic asset!) and the dates you'll be available.

Remember to get your application in in plenty of time, as the more popular jobs get booked up very quickly. And don't worry about getting in anyone's way – people will appreciate the help, even if you're just making the tea and doing some photocopying.

Career calamity

Please help. I think I want to be a teacher, but my careers officer's telling me to become a nurse. What should I do?

Don't always believe what your careers teacher says, for a start! Take a personality test to get a picture of the type of person you are, and what job you're best suited to. Then take a closer look at the jobs that you thought you'd like to do, the jobs your careers teacher recommended, and the jobs your personality test results suggested. See if there's any overlap, look at the skills and qualifications you need to do them, and you'll soon get a clearer picture about what interests you. Start by reading the job ads in newspapers and on websites – for example, Monday's *Guardian* newspaper has a section advertising media jobs. One for a magazine writer might require 'a strong interest in current affairs and proven writing ability'. If you've got that, then this might be the job for you. But if you'd rather watch paint dry than switch on Newsnight, and the last thing you wrote was a shopping list, you'll have to look around to find something that's more suited to your abilities and interests.

If you can't decide which career to go for, you could try taking GCSE or A level subjects that could suit several different careers. Then you can do some work experience and see how you enjoy a taste of each job. Also, don't be frightened of asking for advice – call someone who already has the job you're interested in. Finally, remember you can find out more, on your own, at your local careers centre (the number will be in the Yellow Pages) or at some of the careers websites.

If you've still no idea what career you'd like to follow, ask your teachers or careers adviser for more general advice on subjects to take. If you study those subjects that you're best at and enjoy the most you're most likely to want to work with them: but try to get a solid base that allows you flexibility in your future choices.

Folks hopes

I've always been interested in people – my mum says I'll talk to anyone, anywhere. So I recently got a Saturday job in an old people's home, but I'm not really enjoying it. I thought this was some-thing I'd want to do as a career, but now I don't know what to do. Can you suggest anything?

Don't worry that you're not enjoying your Saturday job. After all, it's good that you're finding out more about your interests before entering the real job market. Even though you're not enjoying working with elderly people, or in this particular home, you still may want a 'people person' job. Use the experience you've gained to look at what the job – and not just the work experience – involves, what it is about it you may like, and what you don't. Use the knowledge to help you decide what job you might be suited to. There are heaps of other careers you can try in this area, without ever going near a Zimmer frame again! Of course, if you find you've gone off 'people jobs', maybe you're a different type altogether. Think of the other things that you enjoy and are important to you and look into other jobs that may suit you.

Money, money, money

I love spending my money on new clothes and CDs, and I've decided I want a job where I rake in the cash. Can you tell me what the highest paid job is that I could aim for?

Sorry to break this to you so bluntly, but you've got it all wrong. It's all very well being ambitious and reaching for the top, but that doesn't necessarily mean you should be obsessed with the salary, too.

OK, you'll want to be earning more than two pounds fifty an hour with a free burger meal thrown in, as slinky new outfits and nights out clubbing don't come cheap. But remember that when you begin at the bottom of the career ladder you're unlikely to start off on a fat cat salary. Also, it's far more important to have job satisfaction than to be earning money in a job you hate. That would soon have you clock-watching until hometime, and depressed like you wouldn't believe.

Sort out your priorities, then you'll be well on the road to sorting yourself out with a happier future. Alternatively, if money really does interest you, you might want to consider a career working with money and making money, such as accountancy, investments or trading (see pages 137–43).

Type i – Creative & Media

Chapter 5

MODEL
or Sitting pretty

The Dosh File

Pay: Starting out – £180 a day (mag shoot) to £15,000 (TV ad campaign)

Hours: 3 to 8 hours a day. Some models only work one day per week!

Working conditions: Crazy to quiet

Perks: Travel, self-employment, meeting people

Effort to get job: 5/5

Stress: 2/5

Glamour: 4/5

Qualifications: None

There aren't many careers books that will tell you how to become a model. That's because although virtually every teenage girl dreams of becoming the new Kate Moss, Sophie Dahl or Naomi Campbell, dreams like this don't often come true. *"We only take on one in 300 people who we consider from postal enquiries, competitions or scouting,"* says Clare Whitlock, Head of New Faces at top agency, Models One.

Even then, only a very few girls have what it takes to become a supermodel. The reality for thousands of others is that they never get beyond small ad campaigns or fashion shoots for local magazines. Millions more will never get signed up in the first place. Why? Because you actually need to look like a model to become one! Still, even some of the best came from humble beginnings. Naomi Campbell grew up in the south London suburb of Streatham, while Kate Moss was 'spotted' by a model agency at an airport, heading off on holiday with her parents.

There are also agencies for many different types of models, like the bigger girl, 'character' models for ads, TV and films, or 'body part' models – people who just show their hands or feet.

It's important to remember that modelling isn't a career for life, as the average length of a model's career is around five to ten years. If you are considering a career in modelling, you'll also have to think about what you'll do afterwards, too.

What You Need

You have to be realistic. If you're only five feet tall, it doesn't matter how good-looking you are, the chances of you strutting your stuff on the catwalk are pretty minimal. 'Traditional' models are at least 5ft 6in, and a perfect size 10–12, with well-proportioned features, good skin, hands and teeth.

You must have bags of patience, as models do a lot of sitting and standing around while not very much happens. And organisation comes in handy, as you must know where to be, and when. Sleeping in instead of attending a photo shoot could be disastrous.

You'll always be meeting new people, so you must be sociable and very confident. Tantrums won't be tolerated, so you should be able to work as part of a team. It's not all about *you*!

Also, models have to look good, so take a

healthy approach to life. Drink plenty of water and eat fresh, healthy food. Plenty of sleep is important, too!

How to Get There

Here's the good news for anyone who doesn't like to study – you don't need any formal qualifications, as it's all about your looks. (Although formal qualifications are always a good idea to fall back on and to get a job when your modelling career is over.) Start by getting seen by a reputable model agency, which is a member of the Association of Model Agents (AMA); send in your details, plus two recent photos of yourself (one should be of your face, the other full length – as natural as possible, preferably no make-up) to the New Faces desk, along with your measurements and an SAE.

"Remember, the photos only need to be Boots-style snapshots," says *Bliss*'s Fashion Stylist, Liz Nowosad. *"Don't spend loads on professional pics – the agency won't need them."*

If they're keen, the agency will call you in for a casting to see if you're suitable. Agencies tend to take on one in four girls they see at this stage. Alternatively, find out when they're open to see

41

potential new models, normally from 10 a.m.–12 p.m. on weekdays.

Remember that reputable agencies will NEVER charge you any money for anything, as they'll stump up the cash if they like you.

We get letters at *Bliss* every week from tearful wannabe models who have got nowhere after they paid a fee for registration or portfolio pictures to less scrupulous agencies. However exciting their offers might seem, you need to be careful. There are agencies who will rip you off.

How I Became A . . . Model by Ruth Spivey

After being spotted at the Clothes Show Live, Ruth modelled part-time until she finished her exams. Now she's a familiar face in magazines like Vogue, and at catwalk shows all over the world.

It was about two months before my sixteenth birthday, and some friends and I had decided to go to the Clothes Show Live event. I'd been the year before and really enjoyed it, as I'm a bit of a shopaholic. To my surprise, I was spotted by two agencies, Models One and Select. It's funny, I knew there were agencies there, but I never thought they'd be interested in me, even though modelling was a bit of a dream. But they had a chat with me, took a Polaroid picture, and said they'd contact me if they were interested. Models One actually phoned that night, and arranged for me to travel to London to meet them. They immediately decided they wanted to take me on – I had no idea what I was doing, but it felt absolutely brilliant. I was so excited.

From there, I started attending castings and doing some modelling during school holidays, travelling to London from my parents' in Hertfordshire. I remember my first job was for some pictures in Shout magazine, and I carried on working during holidays until I finished my GCSEs.

I decided to take a break from modelling during A levels, as it was pretty difficult to combine the two. Anyway, I don't think it's a good idea to take that kind of work too seriously until you're about 18 or 19, as there's a bit of a limit to what you can do. After my A levels, I decided to try modelling full-time, for at least a year. The work's been going really well for the past ten months. I've done some stuff for British and Japanese Vogue and Italian Elle, and I've done quite a few catwalk shows, too. I've thought about going to university, but now I've decided to carry on modelling, trying to be as successful as I can. After all, why stop now?

Related Jobs

Make-up artist: Applies make-up to anyone from models and pop stars to 'real people' at photoshoots, shows, or on movies and TV.

Set designer: Works behind the scenes on TV, movies and the theatre, studying scripts and liaising with the director to create the 'locations' seen by the audience.

Photographer: Takes pictures for magazines, newspapers, books, TV, or even for medical or industry use.

Contacts

Association of Model Agents
122 Brompton Road, London SW3 1JE
Tel: 0891 517 644
Can supply a list of member agencies.

Agencies:

Models One: Omega House, 471 Kings Road, London SW10 0LD
Tel (new faces): 020 7352 8310
Elite Premier: 40–42 Parker Street, London WC2E 5PH
Tel (model enquiries): 0906 888 1188 (higher charges apply)
Select: 17 Ferdinand Street, London NW1 8EH
Tel: 020 7970 5211

Storm: 5 Jubilee Place, London SW3 3TD

Tel (model enquiries): 0906 851 5255 (higher charges apply)

Profile: 12–13 Henrietta Street, London WC2 8LH

Tel: 020 7836 5282

Nevs: Regal House, 198 Kings Road, London SW3 5XX

Tel: 020 7352 9496

Model Team of Scotland: 180 Hope Street, Glasgow G2 2UE

Tel: 0141 332 3951

International Health and Beauty Council (IHBC)

Unit 11, Brickfield Trading Estate, Chandlers Ford,
  Hampshire SO53 4DR

Tel: 02380 271733

Chartered Society of Designers

32–38 Saffron Hill, London EC1N 8FG

Tel: 020 7831 9777

E-mail: csd@csd.org.uk   Website: www.csd.org.uk

Association of Photographers

81 Leonard Street, London EC2A 4QS

Tel: 020 7739 6669

E-mail: general@aophoto.co.uk   Website: www.aophoto.co.uk

Chapter 6

JOURNALIST
or Hold the front page!

The Dosh File

Pay: £7,000 a year (local newspaper reporter)
to £26,000 (senior writer on a top mag)

Hours: 40 hours a week, sometimes in shifts.
Often overtime

Working conditions: Vary considerably, from
quiet office to war zone!

Perks: Travel, freebies

Effort to get job: 4/5

Stress: 4/5

Glamour: 2/5

Qualifications: Usually at least 5 GCSEs (including
English) and two A levels. Majority now have a
degree, but this is more flexible for mags

While journalists are sometimes hated as much as estate agents, traffic wardens or tax collectors, their lives seem pretty cool. All you do is wander into the office, interview a couple of people – maybe even Brad Pitt or Jack Ryder – write it up, then wander home again, right? Well, sometimes, but not exactly. In fact, life as a journalist can be stressful, infuriating, exciting, difficult, boring or fun. But one of the things that appeals to people who take up this career is that every day is different. And it's great to see your name in print!

Many journalists or writers begin their careers as reporters on their local newspaper. Local press can actually provide a great grounding for reporters who might then progress to national newspapers or magazines. It's not all 'cat stuck up tree' stories, you know! Alternatively, some people begin on magazines – from exciting 'trade' press titles like *Plastics & Pipework Weekly*, to the ones you're probably more familiar with, like *Bliss*, *Smash Hits*, *more!*, or *Mixmag*. Here, they'll do anything from writing news and reviews, to bigger reports or real life features, interviews and 'emotional' pieces.

Just be warned — it's often a hard slog from the bottom to the top. And if you work as a freelance journalist, it can be tricky building contacts and getting work accepted. The income isn't always regular, either.

What You Need

Becoming a journalist isn't just about having a tape recorder, shorthand skills or a flashy iMAC. You'll need good English qualifications and word-processing skills. Plus an interest in people and current affairs (for newspaper writers) or anything from pop to movies . . . or even plastic! It's also important to have an eye for detail, persistence, initiative, resource-fulness and stamina, as conditions can sometimes be difficult, or hours irregular. An ability to work under pressure and meet deadlines is also vital.

How to Get There

There are two 'recognised' ways into newspaper journalism:

Direct Entry

Two years training as a reporter on a local paper, straight from school or university. About 40 per cent of journalists begin in this way. Some national newspapers also take on a very small number of graduates each year for their in-house course.

Pre Entry

a A one-year college or university course, approved by the National Council for the Training of Journalists (NCTJ).

b An HND, degree or postgraduate course in journalism.

For magazines, things are a little different. Some magazine writers will have worked on newspapers, or done newspaper courses, but many won't. So where do they come from?

A popular route is through a Periodicals Training Council (PTC) course, but heaps of others simply find their way in through work experience. They plead for work experience, then make the tea and run errands, until someone finally says: "Could you finish off this feature for me, please? I'm desperate!"

How I Became A . . . Journalist
by Jordan Paramor

Having started her career on teen pop bible, *Smash Hits*, Jordan is now a freelance writer for various magazines including *Smash Hits*, *Heat*, *Bliss* and *Empire*.

When I was 18, I really didn't know what to do with my life. So I went to the London College of Fashion and tried out all sorts of things, including design, photography, make-up, styling and writing. My tutor said I should become a writer and I remember thinking, 'There's my life sorted'! But then I thought, 'Oh, how do I do that?'

I decided to get work experience at Smash Hits, as it was my favourite mag . . . and I really loved Take That! I arrived one day, and stayed for six months, doing everything from filing and answering phones to opening the post and even making tea. You really have to be prepared to do anything on work experience.

I started writing various bits for Smash Hits, and generally made a nuisance of myself while I got to know the staff. Then I heard a job was coming up as editorial assistant, and I thought I might be able to get it. So I hassled people for even more work, just to prove myself.

I got the job, but I was terrible at it! I literally had to teach myself to type, and I got the accounts in a right old state! But I absolutely loved it – one day we'd have Boyzone in the office, the next I'd be out interviewing Ant and Dec.

About a year later, a writer's job came up, but I didn't think I stood a chance – about 2,000 people applied! But I spent ages on my application, and continued to work late, learning even more and coming up with ideas. I got that *job, and spent a brilliant year at* Smash Hits *before moving to an older magazine, called* more!. *Eventually I decided to go freelance, and now I write features for different magazines including* Heat, Bliss, Empire *and* Smash Hits. *Being a writer is absolutely fantastic, and I love the freedom and variety that freelancing gives me. I wouldn't change it for a thing.*

Related Jobs

Public relations exec (PR): Promotes, to journalists, anything from teabags to perfumes and videos to events, on behalf of a 'client'. Similar to press officer.

Presenter: Links together items on TV or radio.

Advertising copywriter: Writes the words which appear in advertisements.

Contacts

National Union of Journalists

Acorn House, 314–320 Gray's Inn Road, London WC1X 8DP

Tel: 020 7278 7916   Website: www.nuj.org.uk

Periodicals Training Council

Queens House, 55–56 Lincoln's Inn Fields, London WC2A 3LJ

Tel: 020 7404 4168

E-mail: training@ppa.co.uk   Website: www.ppa.co.uk/ptc

National Council for the Training of Journalists (NCTJ)
Latton Bush Centre, Southern Way, Harlow, Essex CM18 7BL
Tel: 01279 430009
E-mail: nctjtraining@aol.com   Website: www.nctj.com

Broadcast Journalism Training Council
39 Westbourne Gardens, London W2 5NR
Tel: 020 7727 9522
Website: www.bjtc.org.uk (always check website before writing in)

Scottish Newspapers Publishers' Association
48 Palmerston Place, Edinburgh EH12 5DE
Tel: 0131 220 4353
E-mail: info@spes.org.uk   Website: www.spes.org.uk

Institute of Public Relations
Old Trading House, 15 Northburgh Street, London EC1V 0PR
Tel: 020 7253 5151
E-mail: info@ipr.org.uk   Website: www.ipr.org.uk

Advertising Association
Abford House, 15 Wilton Road, London SW1V 1NJ
Tel: 020 7828 4831
E-mail: aa@adassoc.org.uk   Website: www.adassoc.org.uk

Chapter 7

FASHION DESIGNER
or Design dreams

The Dosh File

Pay: £8,000 a year for an assistant pattern cutter to £50,000 at a top fashion house

Hours: Regular if employed, long if self-employed and starting out

Working conditions: Comfortable, but often stressful

Perks: Free clothes, travel

Effort to get job: 4/5

Stress: 4/5

Glamour: 2/5 to 5/5

Qualifications: Usually a degree in fashion design, or similar

Unless you're an even bigger geek than Josie Grossie in *Never Been Kissed*, there must have been times you've slipped on your favourite party dress and thought: I wish I could have designed this! As a fashion designer, that can become a reality.

There are many different kinds of designers – the best work in 'high fashion', designing for individual clients and creating a season's 'look' (creating the style that's 'in' and deciding which colours and materials are right). Names like Vivienne Westwood, Donna Karan, Tommy Hilfiger and Paul Smith are probably familiar. Although not a lot of young designers work in this field – *haute couture* – there are opportunities to work as sketchers or fitters, to get experience.

Because there are so few big names out there, many designers end up in mass-production, with their ideas produced in large quantities for high street chains like Top Shop or New Look, Debenhams or Kookai. They'll often base their ideas on designs from that season's catwalk shows. And they're likely to work according to specific instructions about cost and materials, which sometimes cramps creative flair.

What You Need

There's no point in trying to become a designer if

you don't have any ideas for outfits – so you need to be extremely creative with a great imagination. Plus, you must have an eye for colours, detail, beauty, and you should know what works and what doesn't, while being able to predict trends.

You'll have to be able to sketch your designs, and it's important to build up a portfolio of work (a book showing your best designs) as it helps to land you a job. It's also vital to have great people skills, as you have to be able to talk to the client and find out what they want – there's no point in designing a brilliant new dress, all Velcro and flappy bits, if they really wanted a pair of sturdy work trousers. If criticism sends you into floods of tears, then look for a different job. People aren't always going to like your designs – and they won't always work for the mass market. Technical knowledge is important – you might need to know how certain materials take print, or how some-thing will be affected if it is dyed or machine washed. You're going to need training, too . . .

How to Get There

To become a fashion designer, it's best to enrol on some kind of appropriate course:

Straight after GCSEs

With at least four GCSE passes, you could do a BTEC
First Diploma course in art and design, either at a
further education college or a specialist art college.

After A levels – BTEC National Diploma

With one or more A levels, including art, plus the
GCSEs above, it's on to a foundation course, like
the BTEC National Diploma in art and design,
which teaches you about all sorts of art and
design, from ceramics to photography.

After A levels – HND, degree

After the foundation course, many students do a
textile, fashion or clothing Higher National Diploma
(HND) or degree. You'll probably need three good A
levels and a strong portfolio to get on one of these.

How I Became A . . . Fashion Designer by Judy Galibardy

**Ever browsed through the clothes at Debenhams, or even
your local Tesco? Chances are, you'll have checked out Judy's
creations, as she's a freelance designer for both . . .**

I'd always been interested in design, so I started on a design foundation course, which normally lasts a year, after my A levels. After that, I settled on a three-year degree in fashion textiles at a college near London.

No matter what you've learned at school, they throw it out of the window when you start at college. You learn all the basics, like what will work, how to make clothes, and how the body works with various kinds of garments. For example, it's no good coming up with a fantastic outfit if the hole for someone's head isn't big enough!

During my second year I did work experience, one day a week, at the men's designer, Duffer of St George. Although I was the only girl there it was brilliant fun – I made the tea, did deliveries, copied patterns and even sorted out the buttons for certain clothes! When I graduated, I was lucky enough to get a job working for the street/surf label, Komodo, who produced a lot of the clothes used in the Leonardo DiCaprio movie, The Beach. I started as an assistant, but worked my way up, and eventually designed three seasons of men's and women's clothes for them.

After two years, I left Komodo – now I'm freelance, designing formalwear and casualwear for Debenhams and Tesco, as well as Tesco's trendy streetwear. We have to be continually aware of anything new that's happening. That's important if you want to become a designer, as the marketing *of a new drink or the launch of a new car could influence trends for the next season. I also think you have to be strong-minded – you must know what you want.*

Working as a fashion designer is a lot of hard work, but it's also great fun.

Related Jobs

Graphic designer: Comes up with the 'look' of anything from a new drink's logo to a club flyer.

Book/magazine designer: Lays out the pages, written by the journalist or author.

Interior designer: Plans the 'look' for buildings interiors, from homes to restaurants, hotels to theatres. Also recommends materials, colours, etc. to be used.

Architect: Designs buildings, from railway stations to houses, shopping malls to bus shelters!

Also: Window dresser, set designer, landscape gardener.

Contacts

Chartered Society of Designers
32–38 Saffron Hill, London EC1N 8SG
Tel: 020 7831 9777
E-mail: scd@csd.org.uk

CAPITB Trust
80 Richardshaw Lane, Pudsey, Leeds LS28 8BN
Tel: 0113 239 3355
E-mail: capitb@capitb.co.uk   Website: www.careers-in-clothing.co.uk

Textile Institute
4th Floor, St James Building, Oxford Street, Manchester M1 6FQ
Tel: 0161 237 1188
E-mail: tiihq@textileinst.org.uk   Website: www.texi.org

The Design Council
34 Bow Street, London WC2E 7DL
Tel: 020 7420 5200
E-mail: info@designcouncil.org.uk   Website: www.designcouncil.org.uk

Interior Decorators and Designers Association
1–4 Chelsea Harbour Design Centre, Lots Road, London SW10 0XE
Tel: 020 7349 0800
E-mail: enquiries@idda.co.uk   Website: www.idda.co.uk

Royal Institute of British Architects
Information Unit, 66 Portland Place, London W1B 1AD
Tel: 020 7580 5533
E-mail: admin@inst.riba.org   Website: www.architecture.com

Chapter 8

EDITOR
or Who cares what we read?

The Dosh File

Pay: Around £25,000 a year, after a few years

Hours: 40 hours a week. Often overtime

Working conditions: Comfortable, office-based

Perks: Books!

Effort to get job: 4/5

Stress: 4/5

Glamour: 2/5

Qualifications: Most applicants expected to have a degree

People often confuse writers and editors, but they're definitely not the same! While a writer actually contributes the words to a magazine, newspaper or book, an editor plans the contents, and oversees its preparation. They'll start by deciding what the article or book should be about, according to what they know about the market. Then they'll look around for a suitable writer, who they 'commission' for the job. When the writer hands in their finished words, the editor 'edits' (reads, alters or rewrites) them before they appear in print.

While most magazine and newspaper editors have been writers, most book editors haven't been authors, so it's book editors we're going to look at here (for careers in magazines and newspapers, see Chapter Six: Journalist).The tasks they perform vary according to the size of the publishing company. In a small one, the editor might do everything, from coming up with ideas and reading manuscripts sent in 'on spec', to checking for spelling errors or correcting 'proofs' (first copies of the finished book). In a larger company, the role might be more specialised, or more managerial, with the editor responsible for forward planning, and liaising with other colleagues on the sale of foreign, book club and special sales rights.

What You Need

Just as a pop star should be interested in music, it makes sense for a book editor to be interested in books. If you're interested in a specialist area like films, chemistry, or even gardening, that could help, but a broad general knowledge is often more important. And although you won't be writing the whole thing, you should certainly enjoy writing and have a good command of the English language.

You'll need sound judgement to decide what to accept and reject, and a good imagination, as it's your creative ideas which will be translated into a book that someone wants to read. Plus you should be good at communicating those ideas and dedicated enough to get them actually happening.

These days, computer skills are important, too, as is persistence and an ability to work under pressure.

How to Get There

You don't necessarily need formal qualifications. Many school or college leavers have worked their way up from secretarial or admin jobs, acquiring skills along the way. Even so, most editorial staff are graduates. Specific publishing degree courses are available, at universities like Oxford Brookes, Robert

Gordon and Napier, but practically any degree is acceptable. Foreign languages are also useful.

Publishers will love anyone with relevant work experience. Get as much as you can, and then apply for jobs at publishing houses when you're ready. Trade magazines like *The Bookseller* and *Publishing News* are great for learning about the trade, and give details of jobs available. Copies will be held in your local library.

How I Became An . . . Editor
by Jude Evans

As an editor for Piccadilly Press, Jude's responsible for looking after many youth titles, including the one you're holding in your hands!

After graduating from university, I moved to London and did some temping work for a while. Then I landed a job as PA to the publishing director of children's fiction at Reed Books. A lot of people get into the industry through that route – either becoming a secretary or doing work experience. With work experience, it's all about getting to know people, showing your ability and that you're keen. Then if a job comes up, people will tend to let you know. It's really important to have a passion for books, and most editors have an English degree.

As PA, I was always really enthusiastic. My boss could see that, and after about six months I got a job as editorial assistant. It involved a lot of the repetitive stuff like administration work, but was excellent grounding to learn the basics, like sorting out reprints and briefing covers. I also did as much as I possibly could to help people out, and taught myself to proofread to prepare for an editorial job and to show I was still keen. After about a year I got a job as assistant editor, working on audio and fiction, and did that for another year and a half. Then I managed to get a job as editor at Piccadilly Press, and I've been working there for the past three years, on all kinds of different titles.

I'm the only full-time editor here, as it's quite a small company, and I love everything I get out of it. My favourite part is commissioning authors to write books, as we get a lot of input into that. We kick ideas around until we've got a format we think will work. When you come up with something new and then see that happen, it's very rewarding.

Related Jobs
Sales director: Liaises with wholesalers and stockists to ensure books are stocked by bookshops and websites like amazon.co.uk.

Production manager: Works out costs of paper and printing, deadlines and orders for books, and deals with a chain of people – typesetters, printers and binders – to ensure deadlines are met.

Publicity manager: Ensures journalists are aware of new books on the market, so they can write reviews or features for newspapers, magazines, TV, websites, etc.

Marketing director: Plans the look of a book, and organises promotional displays/signings for stockists.

Foreign rights manager/sales: Negotiates the sale of an author's work for publication overseas.

Also: Book reviewer, author/illustrator's agent, bookseller, librarian.

Contacts

Society of Freelance Editors and Proofreaders
Mermaid House, 1 Mermaid Court, London SE1 1HR
Tel: 020 7403 5141
E-mail: admin@sfep.demon.co.uk   Website: www.sfep.org.uk

Booksellers Association of Great Britain
Minster House, 272 Vauxhall Bridge Road, London SW1V 1BA
Tel: 020 7834 5477
E-mail: mail@booksellers.org.uk   Website: www.booksellers.org.uk

Publishers Association

1 Kingsway, London WC2B 6XD   Tel: 020 7565 7474

E-mail: mail@publishers.org.uk   Website: www.publishers.org.uk

London College of Printing

Elephant & Castle, London SE1 6SB   Tel: 020 7514 6569

E-mail: info@lcp.linst.ac.uk   Website: www.lcp.linst.ac.co.uk

Oxford Brookes University

Gipsy Lane Campus, Headington, Oxford OX3 0BP

Tel: 01865 741111

E-mail: postmaster@brookes.ac.uk   Website: www.brookes.ac.uk

The Robert Gordon University

Schoolhill, Aberdeen, Scotland AB10 1FR   Tel: 01224 262000

E-mail: i.centre@rgu.ac.uk   Website: www.rgu.ac.uk

Napier University

219 Colinton Road, Edinburgh, Scotland EH14 1DJ

Tel: 0131 444 2266

E-mail: info@napier.ac.uk   Website: www.napier.ac.uk

Chartered Institute of Marketing

Moor Hall, Cookham, Maidenhead, Berkshire SL6 9QH

Tel: 01628 427500   Website: www.cim.co.uk

Chapter 9

CHEF
or What's cooking?

The Dosh File

Pay: From £12,000 a year as head chef in a budget restaurant to £100,000 in a top hotel.

Hours: 60 hours a week. Unsociable with shifts

Working conditions: Hot, frantic and noisy

Perks: Er, free food

Effort to get job: 3/5

Stress: 4/5

Glamour: 1/5 to 4/5

Qualifications: None strictly necessary, but college training normally vital

Maybe Jamie Oliver, the famous "Chuck it all in the pan! Pukka!" TV chef has something to do with this job being one of the most sought-after in the hospitality industry. But not all chefs get to work in TV, like our Jamie. Many will work in hotels, restaurants (where Jamie began his career), fast-food outlets, pubs, schools, hospitals or companies, and even . . . prisons! This means some places will need a highly-skilled chef, who's renowned for his or her food or particular dishes, whereas others only want someone with minimal skills.

In a large restaurant's kitchen there's a definite pecking order. The *maître chef de cuisine* is your head honcho – they direct the kitchen staff and manage everything, plan the fancy menus and order supplies. Next comes the *sous-chef* who'll assist, and maybe specialise in certain dishes. Then there's the *chef de partie*, who looks after a certain part of the menu, like veggies or fish, or even sauces. Below them is the *commis chef*, a trainee who'll spend around six months in each section of the kitchen, learning the ropes.

In other places – like schools – the chef's more likely to be skilled at preparing a small selection, but large quantities of food (fish fingers and chips, anyone?). And in bakeries, pastry chefs will produce baked goods like bread, rolls or cakes.

What You Need

Chefs don't just slave over a hot stove. They actually spend ages dealing with people, so good communication skills are important, as is the ability to work in a team. You must be prepared to work odd hours (shift work) and pretty long ones, at that. Many chefs complain of having few friends and a non-existent social life. You'll also need stamina and fitness (this is no desk job) and the ability to perform well under pressure. When your soufflé's collapsed, your roux has stuck to the pan and the cream's just refusing to whip, you mustn't lose your cool.

Although you should love food, you're unlikely to get a job as a chef if you're a cross between Waynetta Slob and Rab C Nesbitt – brilliant hygiene is important. So try to get as much practice as possible, cooking at home for family and friends.

Finally, be prepared to move out of your local area. Sometimes the best jobs could be at the other end of the country.

How to Get There

To start as a chef, it's very useful to gain qualifications, and there are a few ways to do this:

Going to college or university

There are various qualifications in food preparation available, or even specialist degrees. You should then apply to restaurants for work.

Completing a training programme at a restaurant

Here, you can either gain: **a** a qualification through the Hotel and Catering Training Company (HCTC) or **b** a Modern Apprenticeship or National Traineeship covering all the necessary skills. Both include on-the-job training and college study and the bonus is that you've already got a job!

Attending a specific chef school

Competition is tough, but the training's excellent. They generally offer Modern Apprenticeships, National Traineeships and NVQs.

Entry requirements vary, so contact each college for further details (addresses available from

Springboard UK, the Specialist Hospitality and Tourism Careers Advice Service).

How I Became A . . . Chef
by Kat Vanderpump

Kat no longer spends her days chopping tomatoes . . . now she's a *commis chef* at London's trendy Oxo Tower restaurant.

After considering a career in retail management, I decided it wasn't for me. Then I found out about a year long course at a private cookery school called Leith's, in London. I enrolled on that, and decided to get some experience during the summer. So I wrote to a local restaurant, the famous Oxo Tower restaurant on the south bank of the Thames, and they took me on. Work experience is a great way to find out if the job's for you, and as kitchens are notoriously under-staffed, they'll often welcome an extra pair of hands.

One of the worst jobs was preparing tomatoes. Every day I was given this huge box of them, which I then had to blanche, peel and cut into quarters, before de-seeding and finely dicing them. That used to take me about five hours!

After the summer, I did the course at Leith's, which was extremely thorough. Over the year, I learned about everything from preparing fish and different cuts of meat, to making pastry and desserts. When I left, I was lucky enough to be taken on full-time by the Oxo Tower as a commis chef.

Although I went to university and a private college, you don't need to do that. You can actually leave school at 16 and do appropriate NVQs at your local college. But you have to remember that working as a chef isn't like a normal job. You work very, very long hours – sometimes I'll finish at midnight and be back again at 8 a.m. Plus you often get shouted at, so you have to be pretty thick-skinned. And you have to be part of a team, as people rely on you for everything to come together at the same time. I didn't become a chef for the money or perks, but because I love food and the satisfaction I get from seeing it looking wonderful and tasting good.

Related Jobs

Caterer: Organises the food for functions for special events like weddings, birthday celebrations and even pop bands on tour!

Restaurant manager: Ensures the smooth running of a restaurant with their staff, often greets customers and sometimes waits tables.

Food critic: Writes reviews of products and/or restaurants for publication.

Contacts

Springboard UK – Specialist Hospitality and Tourism Careers
 Advice Service
3 Denmark Street, London WC2H 8LP
Tel: 020 7497 8654
E-mail: info.london@springboarduk.org.uk
Website: www.springboarduk.org.uk

Hospitality Training Foundation
3rd Floor, International House, High Street, Ealing, London W5 5DB
Tel: 020 8579 2400
Website: www.htf.org.uk

**Hotel & Catering International Management Association
(HCIMA)**
191 Trinity Road, London SW17 7HN
Tel: 020 8772 7400
E-mail: library@hcima.co.uk   Website: www.hcima.org.uk

Brewers and Licensed Retailers Association
42 Portman Square, London W1H 0BB
Tel: 020 7486 4831 / 09068 443322 (helpline)
Website: www.blra.co.uk

Leith's School of Food & Wine

21 St Alban's Grove, London W8 5BP

Tel: 020 7229 0177

E-mail: info@leiths.com   Website: www.leiths.com

Chef schools:

The Paul Heathcote School of Excellence

3rd Floor, Onwood Building, 207 Deansgate, Manchester M3 3NW

Tel: 0161 839 5898

E-mail: cookeryschool@heathcotes.co.uk Website: www.heathcotes.com

Butlers Wharf Chef School

Cardamom Building, 31 Shad Thames, London SE1 2YR

Tel: 020 7357 8842

E-mail: enquiries@chef-school.co.uk   Website: www.chef-school.co.uk

Barzone – Website with information on careers in pubs and bars.

Website: www.barzone.co.uk

Chapter 10

POP STAR
or Now that's
what I call music

The Dosh File

Pay: £40 a week (or less, when starting out) to £millions at superstar level

Hours: Acts just starting out are lucky to get five hours' sleep a night

Working conditions: Pressurised, frantic and noisy . . . or quiet and lonely

Perks: Free food, clothes, travel (if you make it big)

Effort to get job: 5/5

Stress: 3/5

Glamour: 5/5

Qualifications: None

Who hasn't dreamed of appearing on Top Of The Pops? Or signing autographs for adoring fans and staying in swanky hotels all over the world? The sad reality is that this doesn't really represent life as a pop star. When the Spice Girls started out, they were lucky to get five hours' sleep a night, as they rushed around promoting themselves. This is vital, as people have to see your face if they're going to buy your singles. That means countless interviews with magazines and newspapers, not to mention radio and TV – really not that glamorous when you've already done 47 that week! That's all before you get in the studio to record your new single, or get on stage to promote it with PAs in places from schools to shopping centres. With each band trying to outdo the last, it's a tough life. In fact, it's widely said that only ten pe cent of being a pop star is performing, and the other 90 per cent is taken up by all the tedious things like promotion, recording and travel.

What You Need

There's no set route to becoming a pop star, but talent's important – it helps if you can sing! If you started at a young age, that's also good.

Anyone wanting to make it needs heaps of ambition, loads of practice and buckets of perseverance. After all, if you only ever do one gig, or send your demo tape to one record company, chances are nobody's going to notice you, except maybe the caretaker. And you don't want to be mopping floors for your future.

You should also be interesting, ridiculously ambitious (never take no for an answer!) and incredibly thick-skinned. It's an extremely competitive industry and it's very difficult to make it – be prepared for this and ready to accept countless knock-backs. Oh, and here's the good news for anyone who doesn't like to study – qualifications aren't important.

How to Get There

Many pop stars start at stage school, where pupils get an idea of what it takes to be a celeb, whether that's as a singer, presenter or actor. Possibly the best known is London's Sylvia Young Theatre School – once home to singers including Billie Piper, Emma 'Baby Spice' Bunton and Scott from Five. Others (sometimes seen as more 'serious' musicians) become part of a local band, forget to wash, and strum their guitars at various dodgy venues until some small record label takes notice and possibly signs them up.

Then again, there's people like Britney Spears, Christina Aguilera and Justin from 'N-Sync, who came up through TV shows (the three starred on America's Mickey Mouse Club), TV ads and various acting roles before breaking into the music biz. For some pop stars, getting there has been surprisingly easy. Take Steps, the Spice Girls, and Five, who all answered adverts and went along to auditions. It's a good idea to keep your eyes peeled for such ads – 'Can you sing? Dance? Want to be in a band?' in local papers, but also in the performer's bible, *The Stage*. This weekly newspaper has heaps of adverts for wannabe pop stars, with audition details. You can also try mags like *Melody Maker* and *NME,* or the industry title, *Music Week*. Send your 'demo' (a tape of your songs) to as many managers, producers, journalists and A&R (that's Artist and Repertoire) people as you can find. Who knows, one of them might call you back. Just don't hold your breath.

If you're in a band playing local gigs, invite managers, producers and friends along (you need an audience!) and hope you get noticed in the same way. Even if you don't become the next big thing, you could find yourself as one of Britney's backing singers!

How I Became A . . . Pop Star
by Jessica Simpson

After smash hits including 'I Wanna Love You Forever' and 'I Think I'm In Love With You', 19-year-old Jessica's become a household name worldwide. But even this American super-star didn't have it easy on the road to fame.

I grew up singing – just because I loved it. It was a part of who I was, and I sang everywhere I went. Then, one day, our dance teacher took us all to audition for the Mickey Mouse Club TV show. I eventually got to the final auditions, in Florida, and spent two weeks with Britney, Christina and Justin. But when the moment of truth came, I froze. I realised I didn't have as much experience as the rest of them, and I hadn't done any commercials. They got on the show, but I didn't make it. I still dreamed of making it big, so I got voice lessons, which are very important if you want to become a singer or you can ruin your voice.

After that, it was just fate. When I was 14, I was at a church camp, and met this guy who was starting a record label. I sang for him, and it all began to happen. I made a Gospel record, which was a great experience – then, suddenly, the record company folded. By this stage I was 16, and I decided I was just going to go to school and be a normal kid. But I still had this burning desire to be a pop star. You see, you really have to be driven, and you can't give up.

It was all about connections from there. Somebody from my old record company hooked me up with some people in the business, and I sang live for nine record companies in two days. I didn't even have a demo, because I hated the one I'd made. I eventually ended up with Columbia, my record company, after someone secretly sent them my demo. They offered me a deal, and here I am!

Related Jobs
A&R person (Artist & Repertoire): Searches out, signs and develops acts for a record label.
Record producer: Works with pop stars in the recording studio, to get their songs recorded and sounding 'right'.

Contacts
BMG Records
Bedford House, 69–79 Fulham High Street, London SW6 3JW
Tel: 020 7384 7500

The Stage newspaper
Stage House, 47 Bermondsey Street, London SE1 3XT
Tel: 020 7403 1818
Website: www.thestage.co.uk

Music Week
United Business Media Ltd, Fourth Floor, 8 Montague Close,
 London SE1 9UR
Tel: 020 7940 8500

Musician's Union
60–62 Clapham Road, London SW9 0JJ
Tel: 020 7582 5566
E-mail: info@musiciansunion.org.uk Website: www.musiciansunion.org.uk

Sylvia Young Theatre School
Rossmore Road, London NW1 6NJ
Tel: 020 7402 0673
E-mail: sylviayoung@freeuk.com

EMI Records
EMI House, 43 Brook Green, London W6 7EF
Tel: 020 7605 5000

Sony Records

10 Great Marlborough Street, London W1F 7LP

Tel: 020 7911 8200

Virgin Records

Kensal House, 553–579 Harrow Road, London W10 4RH

Tel: 020 8964 6000

Warner Music

Warner House, 28 Kensington Church Street, London W8 4EP

Tel: 020 7368 2500

Chapter 11

ACTOR
or Lights, camera, action!

The Dosh File

Pay: Around £300 a week (minimum) for a part in London's West End, to £60,000 a year for a top soap role or £millions for a Hollywood movie

Hours: Vary according to role. Usually long, unsociable and irregular

Working conditions: Shoddy to stylish!

Perks: Does possible fame and fortune count?

Effort to get job: 5/5

Stress: 3/5

Glamour: 2/5 to 5/5

Qualifications: None, but many actors are formally trained

Think about famous actors or actresses, and who springs to mind? Katie Holmes or Joshua Jackson? Leo DiCaprio or Kate Winslet? Maybe even Jack Ryder or Jane Danson? Now forget them, because they are a special, showbizzy few. For many, becoming an actor is extremely hard work with long, unsociable hours, and most wannabes never reach the lofty heights of these TV and movie superstars. Some even take jobs waiting tables or serving in shops, because acting work can be irregular and badly paid.

But don't let that put you off, because being an actor is an extremely satisfying career, and there's all sorts of avenues to explore, including TV, films, radio, audio and the theatre.

Television

When our parents were teenagers they had just a few TV channels to entertain them. Now there are countless satellite and cable stations, too.

Film

After massive Brit flicks like *Notting Hill* and *The Full Monty*, there's more and more work in this industry. Many Brit actors have also made it in Hollywood – like Minnie Driver and Kate Winslet.

Radio

The BBC produces hundreds of hours of radio drama each year. And with more commercial radio stations than ever, like London's Capital FM, or Key 103 in Manchester, there's more work for ad voice-over actors, too.

Audio

Audio books, tapes for the blind, comedy cassettes – here are even more openings!

Theatre

There are a lot of national, regional and community theatre companies.

What You Need

You're going to need a lot of talent and imagination. You might be playing a desperate drug addict one week and an elated bride the next, and you won't get far if you play them both the same way!

What else? You should have an absolute passion for your craft, plus ambition, determination and stamina to live your dream. There's masses of competition out there, and not everyone will make it, so you also have to be persistent. Especially as there are fewer parts for women than men. You'll also need to be pretty thick-skinned to get through auditions, or to handle rejection. And performing your heart out and still getting panned by the most savage critics isn't pleasant, either.

Even then, that's not all. You'll need to be flexible to work weird hours (or shifts as bar staff when the money's not coming in!) and be able to set aside a lot of time for learning lines and rehearsing.

How to Get There

As more and more people try to get into acting, experts advise trying to get as many advantages as possible over the next person. One of the biggest advantages you could have would be studying at a recognised theatre school, like the Sylvia Young Theatre School, based in London. You not only have normal lessons, but learn extra skills in acting, singing, and how to deal with the whole industry.

School leavers can also train at drama school, which is open to 17–25-year-olds. All sorts of courses are available, depending on whether you've been to university or not. You'll not only learn all the skills you need, but increase your chances of being spotted by people in the industry who might, just might, want you to dress up as a giant talking peanut for a peanut butter ad. Your first, big break! There are also drama degrees available at universities throughout the UK.

Of course, not everyone is formally trained. Jack Ryder got the part as EastEnders' Jamie Mitchell completely by accident, when he accompanied his mate to an audition and they asked non-actor Jack to audition too! Others might be involved in amateur theatre before going for professional roles, so take part in as many school productions as possible, and join an amateur dramatics society. Also look in the performers' bible, *The Stage*, a weekly newspaper containing news of many upcoming auditions and roles available.

How I Became An . . . Actor
by Natalie Cassidy (Sonia in EastEnders)

As EastEnders' troubled teen, Sonia, Natalie's one of the UK's best-known soap faces. So her tips for the top are going to be pretty cool . . .

When I was eight, my teacher used to write musicals for the school to star in – I remember playing a bee in one, and a Scots bloodhound in another! I got a real buzz out of performing in front of people and making them laugh.

About that time, I'd also started going to Anna Scher, a theatre school, three times a week, after 'proper' school finished. One day, when I was ten, someone came to the school to hold open auditions for EastEnders. I didn't really know what EastEnders was, because I was banned from watching it, but I only had to do some improvisation with my best friend, so it didn't really matter. In fact, I thought nothing more of it until I was suddenly called to the EastEnders studios, in Elstree, for another audition. I went in and read from a script anyway, and then the lady auditioning everyone said I should go home and forget all about it.

A few days later I arrived home from school to find a huge bouquet of flowers waiting for me. I rang Anna Scher and was told I'd got the part of Sonia – it was amazing! The acting profession is huge, and only one in ten actors actually have a job, so I'm grateful to still be in EastEnders, seven years later.

You've got to have talent, stamina and determination to succeed, and I'd say that anyone who wants to follow in my footsteps should definitely be able to do something else, too.

When you make it, it's amazing to be able to do some-thing you love every day – it's just not like work at all.

Related Jobs

Director: Interprets plays or scripts, auditions actors/presenters and conducts rehearsals to achieve the best possible performance.

Producer: The team leader who makes a pro-duction happen, by raising funds, selecting a director, etc. – also a producer has a number of management roles.

Film editor: Edits the raw footage to the director's requirements, often using sophisticated computers.

Camera operator: Films TV shows or movies.

Contacts

Arts Council
14 Great Peter Street, London SW1P 3NQ
Tel: 020 7333 0100
E-mail: enquiries@artscouncil.org.uk Website: www.artscouncil.org.uk

British Actors' Equity Association
Guild House, Upper St Martin's Lane, London WC2H 9EG
Tel: 020 7379 6000 (premium rate line – 60p per minute)
E-mail: info@equity.org.uk   Website: www.equity.org.uk

National Council For Drama Training

5 Tavistock Place, London WC1H 9SS

Tel: 020 7387 3650

E-mail: ncdt@lineone.net   Website: www.ncdt.co.uk

National Youth Theatre

443–445 Holloway Road, London N7 6LW

Tel: 020 7281 3863

E-mail: info@nyt.org.uk

Conference Of Drama Schools (CDS)

1 Stanley Avenue, Thorpe, Norwich NR7 0BE

Tel: 01603 702021

E-mail: enquiries@cds.drama.ac.uk   Website: www.drama.ac.uk

The Stage **newspaper**

Stage House, 47 Bermondsey Street, London SE1 3XT

Tel: 020 7403 1818

Website: www.thestage.co.uk

Sylvia Young Theatre School

Rossmore Road, London NW1 6NJ

Tel: 020 7402 0673

E-mail: sylviayoung@freeuk.com

Anna Scher Theatre
70/72 Barnsbury Road, London N1 0ES
Tel: 020 7278 2101
E-mail: theagency@annaschermanagement.fsnet.co.uk

Italia Conti Academy of Theatre Arts
(Dance & Junior) Italia Conti House, 23 Goswell Road, London EC1M 7AJ
(Acting) Avondale Hall, 72 Landor Road, London, SW9 1AH
Tel: 020 7608 0047
Website: www.italia-conti.co.uk

BKSTS – The Moving Image Society
Unit 5, Walpole Court, Ealing Studios, Ealing Green, London W5 5ED
Tel: 020 7242 8400
E-mail: movimage@bksts.demon.co.uk   Website: www.bksts.com

Chapter 12

VET
or Animal magic

The Dosh File

Pay: £25,500 a year for a new graduate, up to £40,000 after 10 years

Hours: 50+ hours a week. Often on call 24 hours a day, 7 days a week

Working conditions: Sometimes noisy and dangerous

Perks: You're a respected professional

Effort to get job: 5/5

Stress: 4/5

Glamour: 1/5

Qualifications: AAA or AAB at A level (including chemistry and another science), and a vetinerary degree

TV animal shows have suddenly become as popular as ones on making over your home and garden. You can't turn on the TV without seeing Rolf Harris simpering over an injured guinea pig, Trude Mostue stroking an abandoned donkey, or even Patsy 'Bianca!' Palmer getting in on the act at Battersea Dogs' Home. So it's no surprise that everyone wants to become a vet. But the job isn't just about making fluffy kittens better. Vets will work with all kinds of animals, giving medicines, preventing the spread of disease, operating, and advising in other areas, too. Become one, and you'll probably work in a practice with other vets. If your base is in a town, you'll mainly deal with domestic pets like dogs, cats, rabbits and maybe the odd snake or tarantula. In the countryside it's going to be farm animals and equine (horses) which take up more of your time.

If this isn't exactly what you're looking for, there's heaps of other animal-related jobs out there. You could become a veterinary nurse – they're the people who might hold or calm the animals for the vet, carry out tests, and even undertake certain medical treatment and minor surgery.

What You Need

You need to adore animals and be extremely dedicated – being a vet isn't really a job, it's more a way of life. That's just as well, as animals get sick at all times, including Christmas and your birthday. Like Dr Doolittle, you really have to understand animals, as they can't tell you where it hurts or when they're feeling better. It also helps if you're pretty thick-skinned, as putting a sick puppy to sleep isn't a bundle of laughs. If you faint at the sight of a paper cut, think twice about applying, as you're going to see a lot of blood in your career.

Remember that making animals better is only half the job. You have to have brilliant communication skills, as you'll spend the other 50 per cent of your time talking to people.

How to Get There

Spend as much time as possible assisting a vet. You'll have to demonstrate your commitment and experience, as the vet schools won't consider you without it. Also see how a farm works – help out with calving and milking.

Next, you must have some great qualifications.

For A levels, AAA or AAB should do nicely – with two sciences, one of which must be chemistry. Other interests are also important – it helps if you have sporting abilities or musical or creative talent. Even then, you're not guaranteed a place on a veterinary degree course, as there's something like 20 applicants for every place.

Wannabe vets should apply to all six of the UK's vet schools – they're attached to universities in Bristol, Cambridge, Edinburgh, Glasgow, Liverpool and London. The course lasts five years, or six at Cambridge. Contact each one separately for a copy of their prospectus, as entrance requirements vary.

The university courses begin with a couple of years of pre-clinical – that's heaps of theory and science (mmm, lovely). Then comes the clinical work, with more practical experience later on. You're not exempt from working in the holidays, at a kennels, on a farm or in a vet's surgery.

How I Became A . . . Vet
by Jenny Walton

Got a coughing cat or a peaky parrot? Then Jenny, a 'mixed vet', working with farm animals, horses and domestic pets in Yorkshire, can sort it out. Here's her route to the top . . .

I've always loved the company of animals, and I knew early on that I wanted to be a vet. So I made sure I got plenty of work experience while I was growing up, as that's vital if you're going to get on a course at university. Anyone who wants to be a vet should get work at somewhere like a stables, a cattery, a pet shop or a vet's, or help out on a farm. It's also important to be good with people, as you have to be able to explain what's wrong with their animal in layman's terms.

I did A levels in biology, chemistry and physics, and got three interviews, where I was seen by between two and five people who wanted to find out all about me and my experience. I eventually accepted a place at Edinburgh University, and the course lasted five years.

I'm now a mixed vet, doing farm visits, equine and surgery work. I work about eight and a half hours a day, but with extra evening and Saturday surgeries. I also do a duty at a greyhound track for six hours on a Saturday night, and we do shifts where we're on 24-hour call out.

The out of hours work is very difficult – you might get a call out at 2 a.m. from someone who's worried their dog's having a heart attack. Euthanasia – putting an animal to sleep – can also be a very, very distressing time for the animal and the owner, and emotionally trying for the vet, too. But I love working with animals and people. Animals are so important in people's lives – whether in economic value or as pets, and it's great when you can really make a big difference.

Related Jobs

Animal trainer: Trains animals for use in film, TV and other industries.

Groom: Looks after animals such as horses or dogs – grooming, feeding, cleaning, exercising, etc.

Stables/kennel hand: Involved in similar work to a groom.

Contacts

Royal College of Veterinary Surgeons (RCVS)
Belgravia House, 62–64 Horsferry Road, London SW1P 2AF
Tel: 020 7222 2001
E-mail: admin@rcvs.org.uk   Website: www.rcvs.org.uk

British Veterinary Association

7 Mansfield Street, London W1G 9NQ

Tel: 020 7636 6541   Website: www.vetrecord.co.uk

The British Veterinary Nursing Association (BVNA)

Level 15, Terminus House, Terminus Street, Harlow, Essex CM20 1XA

Tel: 01279 450 567

E-mail: bvna@bvna.co.uk   Website: www.bvna.org.uk

Royal Society for the Prevention of Cruelty to Animals

The Causeway, Horsham, West Sussex RH12 1HG

Tel: 01403 264181

E-mail: webmail@rspca.org.uk   Website: www.rspca.org.uk

Animal Care College

Ascot House, 29a High Street, Ascot, Berkshire SL5 7JG

Tel: 01344 628269

E-mail: admin@rtc-associates.freeserve.co.uk

Website: www.animalcarecollege.co.uk

Animal Care and Equine National Training Organisation

Suite 3, St Mary's Mews, St Mary's Place, Stafford ST16 2AP

Tel: 01785 608080

E-mail: acento@acento.org.uk   Website: www.horsecareers.co.uk

Chapter 13

TEACHER
or Think of the holidays!

The Dosh File

Pay: Around £16,000 a year when newly qualified

Hours: Usually more than 40 hours a week

Working conditions: Sometimes stressful and demanding. Often fun

Perks: Er, think of the holidays!

Effort to get job: 3/5

Stress: 4/5

Glamour: 2/5

Qualifications: A degree is a necessity

For many people, leaving school is like winning the lottery. Well, except there's no money involved and you don't usually get into the newspapers. Never again do you have to walk those gloomy corridors, jump at the sound of footsteps behind you, or come home with clothes smelling of stale industrial disinfectant. You're freeeeee! But a few decide they're going to spend the rest of their working lives in the very institution most spent years trying to get away from – they become teachers.

Of course, it's all a bit different when you call the shots. And teaching can be an extremely rewarding career. In fact, anyone who enjoys working with people, inspiring them and helping them to learn, should consider it. But remember, it involves more than waving your arms around in front of a whiteboard and rushing home when the final bell rings. After all, you're responsible for shaping lives, and that's a lot of responsibility. Out of school there's tonnes of admin, extra-curricular activities, and all that marking and planning to do, too.

As well as working in high schools, teachers also work in nursery and primary schools, sixth-form colleges and special schools, independent schools and in adult education (evening classes, Open University, etc).

What You Need

Who's your role model? A singer like Geri Halliwell? A sportsman like Michael Owen or an actress like Katie Holmes? Chances are, you can pick a celeb who inspires you. But there are role models closer to home – yes, like teachers. To be a good teacher, you have to be able to inspire your pupils. If you think hard, you probably know one or two, even now! You'll need the maturity and self-confidence to carry this off, along with imagination and creativity to inspire even the rubber-flicking ones at the back who really don't want to learn. Patience and a sense of humour are also useful. ("Would you like to share that with the rest of the class?" Remember?) And if you thought waiting for your own exam results was hard, wait until you're a teacher. You'll be responsible for all your classes' exam grades – so be ready to handle stress. You must be able to work well as part of a team (you'll even get your own mug in the staffroom!) and also on your own.

You must have a strong interest in a particular subject, along with a good working knowledge of IT. Your pupils will probably be way ahead of you when it comes to the web, and it'll help if you know that a search engine is not a train that looks for missing persons! Excellent time management skills are vital, as you have to be able to plan lessons, and you'll have to be good at administration to get through all the paperwork. Oh, and it helps if you actually like children – even though you might not think that of your teachers!

How to Get There

There are a number of ways to become a teacher, depending on education and experience, but it's worth remembering that any route needs you to have at least a grade C in GCSE English language and maths and science, to begin with. Once you've successfully completed an Initial Teacher Training (ITT) programme, you're awarded Qualified Teacher Status (QTS). This shows you've reached the right standards to teach. Every teacher (unless they're in an independent school) must have QTS. There are two main routes to QTS, through these ITT programmes:

Starting at university (undergraduate):

A three or four year Bachelor of Education (BEd) degree course. This is the most popular route for primary teachers-to-be. (You must have at least five different GCSEs and at least two A levels.)

After your degree (postgraduate):

A Postgraduate Certificate in Education (PGCE) – a one year course following your (usually) three year degree (in the subject you want to teach). This is most popular for high school teaching.

During an ITT programme, you'll learn:

- How to get your knowledge and understanding across to your pupils.
- How to plan, teach and manage a class, plus monitor, assess, report on and account for them.
- Other requirements, such as your responsibilities as a teacher.
- English, maths and science skills, just to check you're up to scratch.

Then, it's off to work . . .

How I Became A . . . Teacher
by Charlie Beyer

After qualifying as a teacher a year ago, Charlie's spent a 'brilliant' twelve months teaching geography to high school pupils in one of Birmingham's most deprived schools.

It's weird, but my mum tells me I've always wanted to teach, as I loved school. I did A levels in maths, geography and sociology, and got a place at Birmingham University, studying geography. While I was at university I made sure I got work experience by going back to my old high school once a week. That wasn't as bad as it sounds, as all my old teachers had left by then! I also got involved in a youth group, which was excellent. I then did a PGCE, which was very different to a degree as you're really thrown in at the deep end to teach in a variety of schools. I finished that last year, and applied for jobs in the Times Educational Supplement. *I've spent a brilliant year teaching in a school in Birmingham – it's in quite a deprived area, and when it comes to league tables, we're almost off the bottom of the scale.*

To be a teacher, I'd say you need a lot of patience and a good sense of humour. A good imagination and a natural ability with children is also important. The best thing about my job is meeting loads of different kids, talking to them on an informal basis, and taking them on trips. We recently took a class to Wales, and some of them had never even seen the countryside before. Sometimes the job gets difficult, as you're teaching a class of 30 and it's hard to give everyone the same attention. There's also a lot of silly paperwork involved. Having said that, I love my job as I'm doing something I've always wanted to do.

Related Jobs
Counsellor: Works with people to help them with decisions or problems – from personal to family, social to mental health.

Nursery nurse: Supervises babies and children and helps them in educational and play activities.

Occupational therapist: Assesses and treats people with physical and psychological problems.

Also: Lecturer/academic.

Contacts
Teacher Training Agency
TTA Communications Centre, PO Box 3210, Chelmsford, Essex CM1 3WA
Tel: 01245 454454
E-mail: teaching@ttainfo.demon.co.uk   Website: www.teach-tta.gov.uk
Free 'Guide to becoming a teacher' available.

General Teaching Council for Scotland
Clerwood House, 96 Clermiston Road, Edinburgh EH12 6UT
Tel: 0131 314 6000
E-mail: gtcs@gtcs.org.uk   Website: www.gtcs.org.uk
Free 'Teaching In Scotland' info pack available.

Department for Education in Northern Ireland
Rathgael House, Balloo Road, Bangor, Co. Down BT19 7PR
Tel: 02891 279537
E-mail: deni@nics.org.uk   Website: www.deni.gov.uk

British Association for Counselling
1 Regent Place, Rugby, Warwickshire CV21 2PJ
Tel: 01788 550899
Website: www.counselling.co.uk
Send SAE for careers info.

**Council for Awards in Children's Care and Education
(CACHE)**
8 Chequer Street, St Albans, Hertfordshire AL1 3XZ
Tel: 01727 847636
Website: www.cache.org.uk

National Association of Nursery Nurses
10 Meriden Court, Great Clacton, Essex CO15 4XH
Send a SAE for info.

College of Occupational Therapists
106–114 Borough High Street, Southwark, London SE1 1LB
Tel: 020 7357 6480
Website: www.cot.co.uk

Chapter 14

RETAIL MANAGER
or Shop talk

Pay: Expect to start on anything between
£16,000 and £25,000 a year

Hours: 40 hours a week standard, but often
longer. Also anti-social

Working conditions: Hectic, on your feet

Perks: Staff discounts

Effort to get job: 3/5

Stress: 3/5

Glamour: 1/5

Qualifications: Some GCSEs useful. Increasingly,
managers have A levels

Although our thoughts of retail are warped by repeats of TV shows like Are You Being Served?, more than ten per cent of the UK's workforce are employed here, so it must be OK! There are certainly lots of jobs around. Anyway, working in a department store needn't be like Grace Bros, and if you're running a supermarket, Dale Winton won't be running up and down your aisles. In fact, most retail staff work in supermarkets (like Sainsbury's or Tesco), department stores (like Debenhams) or high street chains (like WHSmith, Top Shop or Boots) but there are plenty of other retail businesses, including cash-and-carry warehouses and mail order companies. Increasingly it's expanding on to the internet, with companies like amazon.co.uk becoming household names.

As a manager, you'll have to do everything you can to ensure that shopping in your store is a good experience, as well as handling customer queries and complaints, keeping ahead of the competition and maximising profits. You'll probably work Saturdays and, increasingly, nights, Sundays, or Bank Holidays. But you can expect time off and/or extra wages to make up for this.

What You Need

There's no point in becoming a manager if you don't like dealing with people, because that's what this job is all about – both in terms of customers and staff. As the person your staff look up to, you have to be able to inspire them, and convince them that it really is necessary to sweep the shop floor again today, or that the winter coats definitely need re-racking. You have to inspire customer confidence, and although that will sometimes cause you all sorts of hassles, you mustn't explode with fury – a patient attitude with the ability to work under pressure is important.

To succeed, you'll need to have reasonable maths skills, as you'll have to understand about profit, cashflow and balancing the books. And remember, this isn't a comfy sit-at-a-desk-and-surf-the-net type job – you'll be on your feet most of the day. You should also be willing to live anywhere in the UK, as the work won't always be in your home town.

How to Get There

Sales staff don't necessarily need GCSEs, but most managers will have two A levels or equivalent. It is possible to become a manager if you leave school at 16, by working your way up the ladder, through experience and extra study.

Some managers also have a degree – it doesn't matter what subject you study, although there are retail management courses available and this (or something like business studies) could well give you a head start. In any case, graduates are likely to move more quickly up the career ladder.

Many stores, like Sainsbury's and Marks & Spencer, have their own management training programmes.

How I Became A . . . Retail Manager by Ros Williams

As a manager for Sainsbury's, Ros has many years of experience working all over the south of England. She's now manages the supermarket chain's Exeter branch.

When I left school at 18, with A levels in economics and history, I knew I wanted to work in retail. I'd done some work experience at a small clothes store, but I decided to work for someone bigger, so I applied for around six man-agement training schemes with companies including Boots,

Marks & Spencer, Sainsbury's and WHSmith. I was accepted by Sainsbury's, and started on a training programme, which takes between 12 and 18 months to complete.

You work on the shop floor, working the tills, sweeping the warehouse – in fact, doing everything it takes to run the store. If you're later going to ask an employee to do something for you, you have to know everything about their job, so this training's really important. During training you're given a workbook to complete, and you have to manage a project. There are also interviews with a panel of management and an exam at the end of it all.

I really enjoyed the training, and found it very rewarding – it's a great chance to develop all your personal skills. But if you want to become a manager, I'd say it's important to have good interpersonal skills in the first place, as you're always dealing with staff and customers.

After training, I became an assistant departmental manager in Bristol, then moved to London. It can take up to ten years to become store manager, although some university students are fast-tracked to do it in about six years.

In retail, you have a lot of commitments to the store – it's certainly not a nine to five job, and I only get one weekend off a month. But the time flies by and you're always doing something different. A career in retail's really what you make of it.

Related Jobs

Airline hostess (cabin crew): Travels on board aircraft to take care of passengers during flights.

Waitress: Takes orders and serves food and drinks to customers in cafés, bars and restaurants.

Also: Restaurant manager, buyer.

Contacts

National Retailing Training Council
189 Munster Road, Fulham, London SW6 6AW

British Shops & Stores Association
Middleton House, 2 Main Road, Middleton Cheney, Banbury,
  Oxon OX17 2TN
Tel: 01295 712277
E-mail: info@bssa.co.uk   Website: www.british-shops.co.uk

Aviation Training Association
Dralda House, Crendon Street, High Wycombe, Buckinghamshire HP13 6LS
Tel: 01494 445262   E-mail: mail@aviation-training.org

Hospitality Training Foundation
3rd Floor, International House, High Street, Ealing, London W5 5DB
Tel: 020 8579 2400   Website: www.htf.org.uk

Chapter 15

DOCTOR
or Help is at hand

The Dosh File

Pay: From £24,000 a year as Junior House Officer to £54,000 for a GP

Hours: 50 to a staggering 100 hours a week – the subject of continual controversy

Working conditions: They vary hugely – but you're always very busy!

Perks: None

Effort to get job: 5/5

Stress: 5/5

Glamour: 2/5

Qualifications: Usually AAA in A level sciences, plus a degree from medical school

With Casualty the TV show regularly voted *Bliss* readers' favourite programme, there must be a lot of people who fancy being doctors. Still, that probably has more to do with George Clooney in reruns of ER, than Charlie in Casualty. Most doctors work for the NHS, and there are three main types:

Hospital

A hospital doctor begins as a stressed-out and run-off-your-feet house officer, which lasts a gruelling year, before moving up to senior house officer.

General Practitioner (GP)

This is your family doctor who works in a surgery, usually with other doctors, normally somewhere up the road from your house! They deal with all kinds of illnesses and problems.

Public Health & Community Health

Public health doctors deal with preventative medicine and environmental health, whereas community health doctors deal with family planning, hostels, etc. Many doctors do private work in addition to working for the NHS. A number act as consultants

115

and others are occupational doctors – visiting people where they work. Others do research or teaching.

What You Need

If you'd rather analyse the tragedy of *Hamlet* instead of the composition of copper sulphate, then becoming a doctor probably isn't for you, as you need a strong ability and interest in science subjects. You must also have a caring, responsible attitude, and a genuine interest in people and their welfare. Patience is important, as you'll be spending a lot of time with people who are anxious, ill or in pain. And you should be thick-skinned enough to cope with high levels of stress and responsibility. Aside from all that, wannabe docs should be extremely keen and committed, as the competition for medical school places is intense.

How to Get There

It's another of those jobs where you need to be super-brainy. You'll have to have shedloads of GCSEs for starters, plus three A levels, probably all grade A. That's one in chemistry and two from other sciences or maths. Then it's off to university medical school, for a degree course lasting five or six years. It's handy to know that anyone who's missing some science A levels can possibly do an additional university year at the start of their course to catch up. Blimey, you'll be an old woman before you leave!

After finishing medical school you must spend a pre-registration year working in a hospital as a resident junior house officer. After that, you get registered with the General Medical Council (GMC), which allows you to go and seek your fortune.

How I Became A . . . Doctor
by Kate Adams

Becoming a doctor doesn't always mean going to medical school at 18. Kate took a different route into the profession, and currently works as a doctor in a London hospital.

Although most doctors have been medical students from the age of 18, about five to ten per cent come through a different route. I actually did a normal degree, followed by an NHS management training scheme for graduates – so I didn't actually start medical school until I was 26! It's weird, because they're still interested in your A levels when you apply – it's important to have excellent grades in the science subjects. But being older was also an advantage for me, as I had more life experience.

To become a doctor, I think you need to be good with people and have great communication skills. You must also be willing to learn continually – that never stops. The course was hard work and quite intense, but a lot of fun, too – you never forget experiences like helping to deliver your first baby. I even went to the Outer Hebrides, to see what it's like being a doctor there.

I'd eventually like to be a family doctor in an inner city area, so I'm currently completing three and a half years as a house officer. I've so far spent some time in surgery, medical, A&E, and later I'll be doing psychiatry and paediatrics. After that, I'll train as a GP, being attached to a small practice.

Being a junior doctor is extremely hard work, because of the long, anti-social hours. You don't get to see your friends much, and you can say goodbye to the student life. You might start at 9 a.m. on a Saturday and work through to Monday night at 5 p.m., with only five hours sleep. But I love the fact that you're constantly learning, and there's a great human interest factor – you're always meeting different people who are facing different things at different stages in their lives.

Related Jobs

Dentist: Diagnoses and treats problems affecting the mouth and teeth.

Optician: Examines eyes, tests sight, and prescribes glasses or contact lenses.

Pharmacist: Checks the details and safety of prescriptions and dispenses appropriate drugs.

Midwife: Gives care and advice to mums, dads and their babies, before, during and after birth.

Charity fundraiser: Organises events and appeals to raise money for charity.

Also: Physiotherapist, nurse, alternative medicine.

Contacts

British Medical Association (BMA)

England: Public Information Officer, BMA House,
Tavistock Square, London WC1H 9JP
Tel: 020 7387 4499
E-mail: cmay@bma.org.uk   Website: www.bma.org.uk
Scotland: BMA Scottish Office, 3 Hill Place, Edinburgh EH8 9EQ
Tel: 0131 662 4820
Wales: 1 Cleeve House, Cardiff Business Park,
Llanishen, Cardiff CF14 5GP
Tel: 02920 766 277

THE SMART GIRL'S GUIDE TO **YOUR DREAM JOB**

Department of Health

Personnel Department, Room 480D, 4th Floor, Skipton House, 80
London Road, London SE1 6LW

Tel: 020 7972 5398   Website: www.doh.gov.uk

NHS website: www.nhs50.nhs.uk/nhstoday-occupations-doctor.htm

British Dental Association (BDA)

General Office, 64 Wimpole Street, London W1G 8YS

Tel: 020 7935 0875

E-mail: enquiries@bda-dentistry.org.uk Website: www.bda-dentistry.org.uk

Ambulance Service Association

2nd Floor, Friars House, 157–168 Blackfriars Road, London SE1 8EU

Tel: 020 7928 9620

E-mail: asadirect@aol.com   Website: www.ambex.co.uk

General Optical Council

41 Harley Street, London W1G 8DJ

Tel: 020 7580 3898

E-mail: goc@optical.org   Website: www.optical.org

National Pharmaceutical Association

Mallinson House, 36–42 St Peter's Street, St Albans, Hertfordshire AL1 3NP

Tel: 01727 832161

E-mail: npa@npa.co.uk Website: www.npa.co.uk

English National Board for Nursing, Midwifery and Health Visiting

Victory House, 170 Tottenham Court Road, London W1P 0HA

Tel: 020 7388 3131

E-mail: link@enb.org.uk   Website: www.enb.org.uk

Scotland Tel: 0131 225 2096

Wales Tel: 02920 261400

Northern Ireland Tel: 02890 238152

Institute of Charities Fundraising Managers (ICFM)

Central Office, Market Towers, 1 Nine Elms Lane, London SW8 5NQ

Tel: 020 7627 3436

E-mail: info@icfm.co.uk   Website: www.icfm.org.uk

Chapter 16

POLICE OFFICER
or Call 999

The Dosh File

Pay: £16,635 a year during training to
£19,713 after two years service

Hours: Usually 40 hours a week, but expect
overtime and anti-social shifts

Working conditions: Varied – indoor and outdoor.
Sometimes dangerous

Perks: None

Effort to get job: 4/5

Stress: 4/5

Glamour: 2/5

Qualifications: No minimum requirements but a
good standard expected

Is The Bill your favourite TV show? Even if it's not, you'll know that the police help make the world a safer place to live. Well, except in Sunhill, where they seem to spend most of their time chasing petty thieves through run-down estates and then losing them somewhere in the garages around the back.

In all, there are 43 forces in England and Wales, eight in Scotland, and one in Northern Ireland. Police officers prevent and detect crime by covering a 'beat', or pre-assigned area – but that's only a third of their work. In any day, an officer might also direct traffic, deal with a neighbourhood dispute or a missing person, and control someone who's drunk too much or taken drugs. Phew!

Everyone joins the police force as a constable, but there are specialist jobs out there, in areas like the Criminal Investigations Department (CID), dog handling or the river police.

If it's glamour you're after, you won't find it here. A lot of time is spent doing stuff like writing reports or appearing in court. And if you want an easy life, you can forget that, too. Police officers have to provide a service 24 hours a day, which means you'll sometimes have to work weekends, public holidays and even at 3 a.m. in the morning!

What You Need

If your favourite expression is "It fell off the back of a lorry", or you panic when you've lost your purse, then the police force probably isn't for you. That's because police officers need to be absolutely fair and honest, and also calm in a crisis. And if you don't like people, don't sign up, as you'll be dealing with the public every day – and they'll often be stressed, upset or even aggressive. It'll help if you can speak and write well and with confidence. You must also be independent, but able to work in a team, and have good powers of observation and a good level of physical fitness. Be prepared to work long and unsocial hours. At accidents and emergencies you'll see some pretty nasty sights, so a strong stomach and the ability to stand the sight of blood are important. Finally, you must have a smart, conventional appearance, although there are no specific height requirements. Eyesight standards vary between forces.

How to Get There

It's hard to be specific about qualifications, as entry requirements vary between forces, but GCSE English language and maths are important. Every applicant sits the PIR test, an entrance exam which tests various abilities like spelling, checking information, solving numerical problems and your powers of observation.

If university's not your thing, you can enter the force once you're 18 and a half. It's sometimes even possible to join the police cadets at 16 (check with individual forces). Bear in mind that becoming a cadet does not definitely mean you'll become a police officer, and there are a lot of applicants for a few places.

There are also graduate entry schemes, for people who have been to university, and the chance to join an accelerated promotion scheme. Whatever, everyone serves a two-year probation, including training at special centres. After that, you can specialise.

How I Became A . . . Police Officer
by Anna Lucas

Anna knows what it's like to feel the long arm of the law . . . because she's at the end of it! Newly qualified, she's spent a year as a WPC.

Although I worked hard at school and got good GCSEs and A levels, I had no idea what I wanted to do with my life. I decided to do a geography degree at university, and thought I'd probably become an accountant. I did a lot of accountancy temping and hated it – you sit in an office all day, with the same people, so it just wasn't for me.

During my second year at university I got involved in some voluntary community action work, taking young, underprivileged kids on holidays. I really enjoyed that and found it very rewarding, so I started to think about a career in the police force. I went to have a chat with a WPC in the area where I grew up – that's a great idea if you want to find out more. She was fantastic – really enthusiastic and encouraging, and I realised that modern day policing has changed considerably from the old days. It's now a really fantastic career for a woman.

You really don't need any formal qualifications, but it helps to have a strong personality, good interpersonal skills and the ability to reason and listen fairly. You also need a determination to succeed.

I went through quite a rigorous selection procedure, with lots of interviews and physical and mental tests. I finally began training last year, which included 15 weeks on an intense course at a special residential college. Now I'm qualified,

I'd say the worst thing about my job is the shift work – I find nights (10 p.m.–7 a.m.) pretty demanding. But I love meeting all kinds of people from all walks of life, and the job's different every day – you never know what's just around the corner.

Related Jobs

Firefighter: Advises on fire safety and deals with all kinds of emergencies, from road and rail disasters to flood, chemical spills, trapped people or fires.

Private detective: Works in a variety of areas, including tracing missing persons, surveillance and delivering legal documents.

Armed Forces: The Army is Britain's largest employer, but what about the Royal Air Force or the Navy? It's more a way of life than a job and you must have good people skills, be able to follow orders and have a good sense of discipline.

Contacts

Police Recruitment Department

Home Office Police Personnel & Training Unit, Room 510, Home Office, 50 Queen Anne's Gate, London SW1H 9AT

Tel: 0845 608 3000

Website: www.policecouldyou.co.uk

Metropolitan Police Service

Recruiting Centre, 40 Beak Street, London W1F 9RQ

Tel: 0345 272 212

Scottish Executive Justice Department

Police Division, Room E1–4, Saughton House, Broomhouse Drive,
 Edinburgh EH11 3XD

Tel: 0131 244 2156

Fire Services Unit (Home Office)

Horseferry House, Dean Ryle Street, London SW1P 2AW

Tel: 020 7217 8754

Website: www.homeoffice.gov.uk/fepd

The Fire Service College

Moreton-in-Marsh, Gloucestershire GL56 0RH

Tel: 01608 650831

E-mail: library@fireservicecollege.ac.uk

Website: www.fireservicecollege.ac.uk

Association of British Investigators

ABI House, 10 Bonner Hill Road, Kingston-upon-Thames,
 Surrey KT1 3EP

Type iii – Business & Finance

Chapter 17

LAWYER
or Legal eagle

The Dosh File

Pay: Around £16,000 a year as a trainee solicitor up to £30,000 when qualified. Even more for barristers!

Hours: 50 to 70 hours a week. Often irregular

Working conditions: Comfortable – offices, libraries and courts

Perks: Prestige, and good pay if you make it to the top

Effort to get job: 4/5 to 5/5

Stress: 3/5 to 4/5

Glamour: 1/5 to 3/5

Qualifications: 3 A levels (grades A/B) and usually a degree, followed by further training

---

Want to be a lawyer like Ally McBeal (only without the neuroses)? Fine, but banish all thoughts of Hollywood, as many solicitors (one type of lawyer) will deal with far more mundane matters, as they give clients advice on the law. Some deal with all aspects of the law, but others specialise, maybe in an area like conveyancing (the details of buying a house); shipping or construction; accident claims; family law (divorce, etc); or even drafting wills. About three in four solicitors work in a private 'practice' with several partners (other solicitors in the same firm). But others will work for particular organisations, like local authorities.

While a solicitor can legally represent a client in court, they usually pass this on to another kind of lawyer – a barrister (England & Wales) or Advocate (Scotland). It's then the solicitor's job to liaise between them, as barristers rarely deal with the client directly.

The barrister tends to specialise even further, and they're generally the one you see in movie courtrooms, complete with wig and gown, cross examining witnesses and all that exciting stuff. There are about 10,000 barristers currently working in the UK. Eat your heart out, Ally!

What You Need

It's no good standing up in court and getting everyone confused about what you're trying to say, so good oral skills and people skills are important. Confidence is vital, too, along with independence, leadership and the ability to argue logically and calmly – acting or debating skills will certainly come in handy here! You should also be able to express yourself in writing and know your maths. Honesty and accuracy are vital, and you must enjoy solving problems (more than the crossword on the back of a newspaper) as you'll forever be checking facts, researching and analysing.

Those who get jobs also tend to have a good work experience record, and all-round 'life experience'. So if you've travelled, held an important post at university, or even been head of the computer geek club, you're more likely to get a job. It'll help if you're determined, as it can feel like you're taking forever to qualify.

Finally, if you're the school gossip you won't make a good lawyer. Start whispering about your clients' cases and you wouldn't believe the trouble it'll get you in. Being discreet is vital.

How to Get There

Most wannabe lawyers are graduates, so there's no escaping the need for a good brain. The usual qualifications are 3 A levels (As and Bs) and a degree (2(i)). Competition to even get on a university law course is fierce – there are around 21,000 applicants for around 16,000 places each year. After that, anyone who hasn't studied law needs to take the Law Society's common professional examination (CPE). What you do next depends on whether you become a solicitor or barrister.

Solicitor

Next up for you is the Legal Practice Course (LPC) in England and Wales, or the Diploma in Legal Practice (Scotland), which lasts one or two years (full-time vs part-time) at one of many colleges or universities. After that, you still might not get a job as a solicitor, as the number of people completing the course is far greater than the number of training contracts (formerly called 'articles') available at solicitors. If you're lucky, an on-the-job training contract lasts two years.

Barrister

For barristers-to-be, next up is a Bar Vocational Course (BVC) at one of the four Inns Of Court School Of Law, followed by a 12-month pupilage at the Bar (apprenticeships to do court work). In the first six months you'll research cases and draft documents, and in the second six months you can actually accept 'briefs' (jobs for a client). This differs slightly in Scotland. However this is probably even more difficult to get into than being a solicitor. There are many more applicants than there are places available.

How I Became A . . . Barrister
by Richard Posner

Order! Order! Richard's dreamed of being a barrister since he was eight. Newly qualified, he recommends getting heaps of work experience if you want to succeed.

Even when I was small, I loved the idea of wearing a wig in court! So, when I turned 14, I was very excited to sit in the public gallery in a criminal court. I used to go there whenever I could during my holidays.

133

Later, I got work experience at a barrister's chambers – you enter into a mini-pupilage, shadowing the barristers and doing a lot of admin work in the clerks' room. I can't recommend it enough, as you get such a feel for the job.

I did my A levels – the subjects don't matter, as long as you get good grades – followed by a law degree at the University of Northumbria in Newcastle, which was a lot of hard work. Next, I got on to a 12-month Bar vocational course in Newcastle, and now I am just completing a 12-month pupilage in Birmingham. My work experience definitely helped me get that. It's really exciting, as I'm currently assisting in a drugs conspiracy case. Technically I'm qualified as a barrister and in two months, when I've finished my pupilage, I'm going to apply to the Army legal services.

To become a barrister, I'd say you need a lot of self-confidence, and you have to be hard-working and committed. It also helps if you're responsible with your finances, as you effectively end up running your own business.

More than half the barristers out there these days are women, and I reckon it's now a brilliant career for anyone. The old-school sexual discrimination is rapidly disappearing – in fact, faster than in most other professions.

The worst thing about this job is the long hours and evening work, but I love the job, and the status it gives you. The independence and salary are quite nice, too!

Related Jobs

Civil servant: Works for the government in one of many departments and agencies, like the Ministry of Defence, or the Department of Health and Social Security, or the Department of Environment. The largest group is Administrative Staff, responsible for policy (at the top) to answering enquiries (at the bottom).

Politician: There are only about 660 Members of Parliament, each representing a constituency in Britain. All have another career to support them, where necessary.

Contacts

Law Society

Information Services Team, Ipsey Court, Berrinton Close, Redditch,
  Worcestershire B98 0TD
Tel: 01527 504 455
Website: www.lawsociety.org.uk

Law Society of Scotland

Legal Education Department, 26 Drumsheugh Gardens,
  Edinburgh EH3 7YR
Tel: 0131 226 7411
Website: www.lawscot.org.uk

Inns of Court School of Law
4 Grays Inn Place, Grays Inn, London WC1R 5DX
Tel: 020 7404 5787
E-mail: bvc@icsl.ac.uk

Faculty of Advocates
Parliament House, Edinburgh EH1 1RF
Tel: 0131 226 2881

Civil Service (Careers)
General Enquiries, capita, Innovation Court, New Street, Basingstoke,
  Hants. RG21 7JB
Tel: 01256 869 555

Chapter 18

ACCOUNTANT
or Money, money money . . .

The Dosh File

Pay: From £9,000 a year as a trainee up to £26,000 when newly qualified

Hours: 40 hours a week, but often longer during the tax season

Working conditions: Comfortable – office-based

Perks: None

Effort to get job: 3/5

Stress: 3/5

Glamour: 1/5

Qualifications: Good GCSEs and three A levels. Many have a degree

Accountants are often portrayed as being boring, but it's not the job that makes someone boring. After all, there are plenty of boring pop stars or models! So if you love number-crunching, maths and dealing with figures, accountancy could be for you. In general, accountants check details of other people's financial transactions and/or help companies budget their cash while ensuring the money's spent properly. Some accountants will specialise in one particular area – like taxation or mergers and takeovers, and some will work in a particular industry – maybe the music industry or the NHS.

Despite its media reputation, accountancy is often varied – you'll be meeting different people and could be doing all kinds of different jobs! If you don't like uncertainty and you're keen to have everything balance itself out, accountancy is a very rewarding profession.

What You Need

You'll have to be good with numbers – and that doesn't just mean deciding how many people you're going to invite to your end-of-exams party. You have to enjoy looking at them every day without going bonkers, too! You must also be able to think on your feet and use computers. And you must have a logical mind that's happy paying attention to detail and analysing things.

Finally, because you're going to be explaining someone's finances to them in layman's terms, you have to be able to work well with people.

How to Get There

You need a minimum of five GCSEs, including English language and maths, plus two or three A levels at grade C or above (subjects like business studies and maths are recommended). About five per cent of accountants then train directly from A levels, although you'll need a degree to enter The Institute of Chartered Accountants of Scotland. Most study for a degree, or complete an accountancy foundation course, to become a member of the Institute of Chartered Accountants. More than 75 per cent of entrants into accountancy now have above a 2(ii). The good news is that the degree can be in any subject – not just maths or accountancy.

Three to five years of on-the-job training follows (95 per cent of trainees now have degrees), along with professional exams before joining an Institute. Be warned – training and the exams are tough, but you finish up with a professional qualification and good prospects in a very rewarding job.

How I Became An . . . Accountant
by Annie Jones

If your books need balancing or your money's in a muddle, call Annie! She's just qualified as a corporate accountant for the NHS.

When I was younger, I didn't know what I wanted to do as a job. Although I'd done some work experience at 15, it hadn't given me any more ideas, so I chose science A levels because I enjoyed the subjects. After those, I got a place studying biochemistry in Birmingham. When you become an accountant, it really doesn't matter what you've studied.

I knew I was interested in the health service, so I got a general administration job, just to see what it was like. I only did filing, data input and answering the phones, but it gave me a really good insight, and persuaded me that was where I wanted to work.

I applied for a place on a graduate training scheme in financial management in the Health Service, and got accepted – I was definitely helped by the experience I already had. With the scheme you actually get to apply for a job, then get trained at the same time. At the end, you take some exams and, hopefully, qualify as an accountant.

During my training I've worked in a hospital in the home counties, which has been really interesting. One of the projects I'm currently working on is the rebuilding of an intensive care unit – I have to assess what's achievable with the money available, and that's been great fun. On the down side, there's a lot of monthly, routine work which is sometimes quite boring.

To do this job, I'd firstly say you need to be good with numbers. But you must also be able to deal with people, as the communication of your ideas, and what the figures mean, is of vital importance.

After three and a half years of training, I have finally qualified, and I can't wait to see what I can do next.

Related Jobs

Stockbroker: Advises clients on which stocks and shares to buy and sell on the Stock Exchange, then carries out the transactions (known as trading).

Bank manager: Interviews customers, assesses

financial risk and ensures the bank runs smoothly and efficiently.

Economist: Deals with the organisation, use and distribution of the world's resources in a variety of organisations, from government to large industries and consultancies.

Insurance underwriter: Decides whether to accept a risk on insuring people or property and calculates the amount to be charged.

Secretary/Office manager: Carries out general office admin duties and arranges meetings and conferences.

Also: Management consultant, events organiser.

Contacts

Institute of Chartered Accountants in England & Wales (ICAEW)

Student Recruitment, Gloucester House, 399 Silbury Boulevard, Central Milton Keynes MK9 2HL

Tel: 01908 248100   Website: www.icaew.co.uk

Institute of Chartered Accountants of Scotland (ICAS)

27 Queen Street, Edinburgh EH2 1LA

Tel: 0131 225 5673

Website: www.icas.org.uk

Securities Institute Services Limited
Centurion House, 24 Monument Street, London EC3R 8AQ
Tel: 020 7626 3191
Website: www.securities-institute.org.uk

Chartered Institute of Bankers
90 Bishopsgate, London EC2N 4DQ
Tel: 01227 762600
E-mail: institute@cib.org.uk   Website: www.cib.org.uk

Institute of Economic Affairs
2 Lord North Street, London SW1P 3LB
Tel: 020 7799 3745
E-mail: iea@iea.org.uk   Website: www.iea.org.uk

The Association of British Insurers
51 Gresham Street, London EC2V 7HQ
Tel: 020 7600 3333
Website: www.abi.org.uk

Institute of Business Administration
16 Park Crescent, London W1B 1AH
Tel: 020 7612 7028
E-mail: sposs@icsa.co.uk   Website: www.ibauk.org

Chapter 19

SCIENTIST
or Why does it happen?

The Dosh File

Pay: From £12,000 a year straight after graduation, to £50,000 by the time you're middle-aged!

Hours: Could involve long or unsocial hours

Working conditions: Comfortable but possible ethical dilemmas

Perks: None

Effort to get job: 4/5

Stress: 2/5

Glamour: 2/5

Qualifications: Degree

When someone mentions scientists, most of us can't help thinking of mad professor-types in white coats, working with racks of test tubes foaming with multicoloured liquids.

OK, there are some scientists like this. But 99.99 per cent look just like you and me, and work across many areas – solving problems, developing products and carrying out research. So while one clever boffin might be finding a cure for cancer, another could be creating a new kind of plastic. And you won't find too many foaming test tubes in their laboratories!

Some of the different kinds of scientists out there include (but are definitely not limited to):

Audiological scientist: Looks at people's hearing ability, to help treat hearing problems.

Biomedical scientist: Carries out investigations on human samples to treat or prevent diseases or illnesses.

Forensic scientist: Provides scientific evidence for use in court.

Product development scientist: Takes ideas for new products and develops them to a point where they can be manufactured.

Research scientist: Increases scientific knowledge by developing theories and conducting experiments.

Basically, if you think you can research it, there's probably a scientist out there doing so right now! And next time it could be you!

What You Need

If you don't have a natural curiosity to find out more about things, how they work, or why they respond in a certain way, then a job as a scientist probably isn't for you. After all, if you think you dream of being a rocket scientist, but don't also dream of taking a rocket apart to see how it works, you're not going to have much fun in that job.

But if that's you to a tee, and you're also extremely patient and self-motivated, able to work on your own or as part of a team, then maybe this is the career for you. Of course, it'll also help if you can communicate your ideas effectively – there's no point in researching something if you can't tell everyone the news about what you've discovered!

How to Get There

Although it's difficult to generalise across such a huge

146

field, the vast majority of – if not all – scientists have been to university and studied for a relevant degree. This could include physical/ mathematical/ applied science, biochemistry, biomedical science, biology, chemistry, physics or environmental science . . . and more! This is sometimes followed by an MSc or PhD. For example, to become an audiological scientist, you'll need a relevant degree and a PhD or MSc in audiological science. If you fancy being a forensic scientist, you'll need an MSc or diploma in forensic science. This is usually followed by on-the-job training.

How I Became A . . . Scientist
by Wendy Bickmore

Wendy is a senior scientist working in the fast-moving and sometimes controversial world of human genetics . . .

At school, I was always more interested in biology than anything else, so I did A levels in biology, chemistry and physics. Then our teacher started telling us about genetics and DNA, which I thought sounded really exciting. At that stage, I was pretty sure I wanted to be a doctor – but was persuaded to do a four-year biochemistry degree at Oxford

University, thinking I could always become a doctor later.

As it turned out, I loved my degree, which included a whole year in a real laboratory, working alongside real scientists – you were given your very own project to research.

Once I got my degree, I decided to do a PhD. A PhD is like an apprenticeship – you spend three years in someone's lab, where they train you in the various techniques they're using, and teach you how to think about certain science questions, and how to write up your answers.

After seven years of studying, I finally got my first job as a scientist, basically working on someone else's idea, for about five years. Now I'm a senior scientist with the Medical Research Council in the human genetics unit. I run my own lab, researching how DNA is organised.

It's very exciting, as everything's advancing so quickly – five years ago, I'd never have believed we'd be able to do what we can do now! And I love the feeling of freedom you have as a scientist. This all makes up for the insecurity you sometimes have at the start of your career. Oh, and the pay's OK, but becoming a scientist is never going to make your fortune!

Related Jobs
Food technologist: Develops new products and processes, or modifies existing ones related to food and its manufacture.

Pharmacologist: Investigates drugs and chemicals and researches drug development.

Contacts

British Society of Audiology
80 Brighton Road, Reading, Berks. RG6 1PS
Tel: 01189 660622

British Pharmacological Society (BPS)
16 Angel Gate, City Road, London EC1V 2PT
E-mail: admin@bps.ac.uk   Website: www.bps.ac.uk

Institute of Biomedical Science
12 Coldbath Square, London EC1R 5HL
Tel: 020 7713 0214   Website: www.ibms.org

Medical Research Council
20 Park Crescent, London B1N 1AL
Tel: 020 7636 5422   Website: www.mrc.ac.uk

Forensic Science Society
Clarke House, 18a Mount Parade, Harrogate HG1 1BX
Tel: 01423 506068
Website: www.forensic-science-society.org.uk

Chapter 20

COMPUTER PROGRAMMER
or Click here to continue!

The Dosh File

Pay: £12,000 a year as a graduate trainee, to £24,000 as a senior programmer

Hours: 40 hours a week, not always 9 a.m.–5 p.m.

Working conditions: Comfortable desk job

Perks: None

Effort to get job: 4/5

Stress: 2/5

Glamour: 1/5

Qualifications: GCSEs upwards. Many have a degree

These days, you can barely do anything without the help of a computer. Even though you might not realise it, everything from microwaving a pizza to booking a cinema ticket or setting the video involves using one. Which means there are plenty of jobs around in information technology, or IT.

A computer programmer is someone who writes – and sometimes maintains – the software in a particular computing language to make a computer perform a task. Different kinds of programmers will specialise in different areas using different languages such as C, FORTRAN or LISP.

A systems analyst will usually decide exactly what needs to be done before enlisting the help of a programmer. For example, they'll decide what the booking system for a new hotel chain must do, before the programmer makes it happen. A programmer might even make a flight simulator work in the same way as an actual plane.

In general, you'll either work for a specific IT company, or in the IT department of an organisation.

These days, there's also a lot of call for a specific kind of computer programmer – the website designer, who will create internet home pages like the excellent Dawson's Creek website (www.dawsonscreek.com)

or the popular e-mail website, Microsoft Hotmail (www.hotmail.com). Another important field is in games design or programming. How would you feel about creating the next Tomb Raider?

What You Need

If setting the video or programming a mate's number into your mobile's memory does your head in, skip the idea of becoming a computer programmer. You must have a logical mind that can think in great detail, and you must be happy solving problems. Plus you should be able to see a project through from start to finish, on your own or as part of a team, and be able to communicate clearly and effectively.

And make sure you can keep up with changes in computer and website technology. It's a fast-moving industry!

How to Get There

Following GCSEs, (you'll certainly need English and maths), you could think about a BTEC National Diploma/Certificate in information technology or computer studies. You could also look at A levels in computing or maths, as these will also be useful.

Many people in computing have degrees,

although it is possible to get into the industry with lesser qualifications. There are plenty of Higher National Diplomas (HNDs) and degrees in IT and computing available (everything from computer studies to information systems or software engineering). It's a good idea to see what past students have gone on to do with their lives before you commit yourself to a particular course!

You can also find training in the workplace – many companies run their own training programmes.

How I Became A . . . Computer Programmer
by Megan Robertson

A self-taught, self-confessed computer addict, Megan developed computer software, before becoming webmaster of a college website.

Computing wasn't what I originally intended to do with my life. At school I did science A levels, followed by a degree in botany.

But when I met my boyfriend, he was already into computing. I thought 'If I can't beat him, I'd better join him', so I started teaching myself programming, and I eventually got a job in a software house, writing software for stock control systems. That might sound weird, but a lot of people in this industry don't have formal computer training. They start off playing around on computers, and then just teach themselves.

I started getting into HTML – the web programming language – in the early 1990s, and managed to earn a living as a freelance web designer. I worked on the Nicorette anti-smoking site, plus others including the Halifax Building Society and Compaq computers.

A lot of people assume computing's a boy thing, because they play a lot of computer games. But with the creativity involved, there's actually a lot of scope for girls.

To do my job, you need a strong creative streak, as you have to be able to dream something up before you can make it happen. And you must have a logical mind and good attention to detail – computers are very stupid unless you can tell them what to do.

Now I'm the webmaster for the website at South Cheshire College. That means I'm responsible for the content, structure and appearance of its website. I love the fact that I can stick my nose into everything and share information with people. Sometimes the hours are a bit long, but the fun I have more than makes up for that. I reckon you should always follow what you really enjoy – if you enjoy it, you'll also pick up how to do it along the way.

154

Related Jobs

Systems analyst: Uses problem-solving skills to plan and develop computer systems for organisations.

Contacts

British Computing Society

1 Sanford Street, Swindon, Wiltshire SN1 1HJ

Tel: 01793 417417

E-mail: bcshq@bcs.org.uk   Website: www.bcs.org.uk

Institute of Analysts and Programmers

Charles House, 36 Culmington Road, London W13 9NH

Tel: 020 8567 2118

E-mail: dg@iap.org.uk   Website: www.iap.org.uk

Information Technology Industry Training Organisation

16 Berners Street, London W1T 3LN

Tel: 020 7580 6677

Website: www.e-skillsnto.org.uk

British Interactive Multimedia Association

Briar Lea, Southend Road, South Green, Billerricky, Essex BM11 ZPR

Tel: 020 7436 8250

Chapter 21

ENGINEER
or It'll never work . . . will it?

The Dosh File

Pay: From around £16,000 a year for newly qualified graduates.

Hours: 40 hours a week

Working conditions: Can be cold, dirty and LOUD! From labs, to building sites, to offices

Perks: None

Effort to get job: 3/5

Stress: 3/5

Glamour: 1/5

Qualifications: From BTEC National Diploma to degree

Never met an engineer? That's strange, because there are half a million of them in the UK, working in all kinds of areas, from bridges to aeroplanes, computer systems to chemicals. But what do they do?

Well, they "plan, design, construct, maintain and research on projects", according to The Institution of Civil Engineers. The projects they work on can be extremely large, like the Channel Tunnel, or very small, like traffic calming.

So, if you think about it, we're all affected by engineering, every second of every day of our lives. There are not many jobs which do that! Here are just a few of the different fields:

Aeronautical Engineering: Planes, helicopters, etc.

Chemical Engineering: Oil, chemicals, pharmaceuticals, food, etc.

Civil Engineering: Construction – foundations, energy, transport, water. (Everything from dams to sewage works, houses to roads.)

Electrical & Electronic Engineering: From power stations to microprocessors.

Marine Engineering: Ships, oil platforms, submarines, etc.

Mechanical engineering: All kinds of machinery — the biggest sector.

The good news is, even if you get bored of engineering, it's widely seen as a 'transferable' skill, so engineers can also make very good business people, marketing managers or lecturers, to name a few alternative careers.

What You Need

This really depends on which level you want to aim for, but you'll need to be good at solving problems and enjoy working with figures. In addition, anyone wanting to become a chartered engineer will need good academic ability, and a sound approach to problem-solving.

You must also be good at working with people. Teamwork is really important in this career, so it's no good if you don't get on with your workmates. And you must have a lot of patience and good interpersonal skills. Computer literacy is vital, too.

How to Get There

Many engineers are university graduates, others have BTEC or equivalent diplomas. After that, you're trained on the job to reach professional standards, for example those of the Institution of Civil Engineers. These are very important as they show you're technically OK to do the job!

There are three grades of professional qualification, no matter what kind of engineer you become: chartered engineer (at the top), through to incorporated engineer and engineering technician.

Each grade requires different qualifications:

Chartered engineer: They study engineering to degree level and receive training in the first few years at work. They mainly work in construction and manufacturing industries, leading teams, and are at the forefront of knowledge and innovation.

Incorporated engineer: They study engineering to BTEC Higher National Diploma level, and are then trained in the workplace. It takes five years of training and experience to get this title. They're often team leaders solving engineering problems.

Engineering technician: They study to BTEC National Diploma level and are then trained in the workplace where they put their knowledge to use.

How I Became A . . . Civil Engineer by David Puttock

Work experience at school encouraged David to become a civil engineer. He now ensures buildings don't "blow over in the wind or fall down", as he explains it!!

When I was 15, I started doing a Saturday job assisting a civil engineer. I only lugged his equipment around, but it got me thinking about my future. I enjoyed being out and about, instead of stuck behind a desk all day. Plus, I knew that if I studied civil engineering at uni, there would probably be a job at the end of it!

I did A levels in maths, physics and chemistry, before starting a civil engineering degree at Sheffield University.

In my second year, I got a summer job with London Underground, working on the Jubilee Line extension project. I was just a general office boy, but they took me back when I finished university – as soon as you qualify, you can actually call yourself a civil engineer. I worked there for a couple of years before moving to a different company.

While architects come up with the basic plans for a building, it's a civil engineer's job to make sure it doesn't blow over in the wind or fall down, so I get great satisfaction from being able to drive past a building whose design I've actually worked on. OK, I don't like writing reports, but everything else makes up for that.

To get my job, you definitely need to be good with figures, but you also need good communication skills as you'll have to chat to anyone from the client to architects or builders.

Although there were only about five girls on my course, out of 90 people, things are definitely changing. There's still some stereotypical attitudes around, but I reckon it's a great career for anyone!

I'd love to be able to design something like the Sydney Opera House. Maybe, one day, I will.

Related Jobs

Land surveyor: Measures and charts physical features of the earth so maps can be drawn. Other kinds of surveyor include general practice (auctioneering and estate agency), aerial surveyor, archaeological surveyor, quantity surveyor, and more.

Estate agent: Represents a property owner to sell their residential or commercial property or land.

Also: Developer, planner.

Contacts

Civil Engineering Careers Service

Institution of Civil Engineers, 1–7 Great George Street,
  London SW1P 3AA

Tel: 020 7222 7722

Website: www.ice.org.uk

Construction Industry Training Board (CITB)

Bircham Newton, Kings Lynn, Norfolk PE31 6RH

Tel: 01485 577577

E-mail: resource@citb.org.uk   Website: www.citb.org.uk

Engineering Council

10 Maltravers Street, London WC2R 3ER

Tel: 020 7240 7891

E-mail: info@engc.org.uk   Website: www.engc.org.uk

Institution of Structural Engineers

11 Upper Belgrave Street, London SW1X 8BH

Tel: 020 7235 4535

E-mail: mail@istructe.org.uk   Website: www.istructe.org.uk

Women's Engineering Society

2 Queen Anne's Gate Building, Dartmouth Street, London SW1H 9BP

Tel: 020 7233 1974

Architects and Surveyors Institute

St Mary's House, 15 St Mary Street, Chippenham,

Wiltshire SN15 3WD

Tel: 01249 444505

E-mail: mail@asi.org.uk   Website: www.asi.org.uk

Chapter 22

SECRET SKILL TO JOB THRILL!
or When your hobby can be your future

This chapter is pretty cool. Like the hidden track on the end of a Robbie Williams album, it's here to add a little extra to everything that's gone before. See, although you'll almost definitely fit into one of the four types shown in the previous 16 chapters, you might be also thinking: "But I'm brilliant at ballet/playing the violin/taking pictures/playing tennis," (delete as appropriate, unless you're a complete poser), "so can't I do that as a job?"

The answer, of course, is: Yes, you probably can, if you're good enough, as there are thousands of people in the UK who have developed their teen talent or hobby into a full-time job.

So, what's to stop you doing the same? It's a competitive field, and you have to be dedicated to make it, but if you fancy being the next Anna Kournikova, Michael Flately or Bruce Weber, you've come to the right place . . .

DANCER

Being a talented dancer involves a little more than throwing your arms around to the latest garage hit at your local nightclub. But if Mum's been driving you to dance classes every Saturday for as long as you can remember, you've been doing shows and exams, and you've been told by people in the know that you have 'talent', then why not think about doing it professionally?

Most professional dancers have had years of training in 'theatre' dance, and the amount of work out there is limited. But there's no reason why you shouldn't trip the light fantastic in one of the three main areas – ballet, contemporary or musical theatre.

As well as being an excellent dancer (of course!) you'll also need to be artistic, committed and determined.

As for the training, ballet students should attend a recognised residential school, like the Royal Ballet School, from the age of 11 to 18. Other dancers usually need to complete a three-year full-time course – The Council for Dance Education and Training (CDET) provides a list of schools (send an SAE).

Even if you don't fancy being right in the limelight, you could become a dance teacher, therapist, or even teach Steps their, er, steps as a choreographer. The demand for dance teachers is much higher than performers, as more and more people want to pick up the skills, even if it's just for fun.

Contacts

Council for Dance Education and Training (CDET)
Studio Eight, The Glasshouse, 49a Goldhawk Road, London W12 8QP
Tel: 020 8746 0076
Website: www.cdet.org.uk

Circomedia (Centre for Contemporary Circus & Physical Performance)
Kingswood Foundation, Britannia Road, Kingswood, Bristol BS15 8DB
Tel: 0117 947 7288
E-mail: info@circomedia.demon.co.uk Website: www.circomedia.co.uk

Royal Academy of Dancing
36 Battersea Square, London SW11 3RA
Tel: 020 7223 0091
E-mail: info@rad.org.uk   Website: www.rad.org.uk

Royal Ballet School
155 Talgarth Road, Barrons Court, London W14 9DE
Tel: 020 8237 7100

ARTIST OR PHOTOGRAPHER

If your talent lies in taking pictures – or making them! – then maybe you can become a professional artist or photographer. Of course, there's far more to each of these areas than simply being able to use a camera, draw, sculpt, or put a couple of sheep in formaldehyde (stand up, Damien Hirst) but if you're good – really good – then why shouldn't you give it a go?

On the downside, only the most successful artists are able to support themselves solely through the sale of their works. It will help if you attend university or art school to get together a portfolio of your work (a special book showcasing your best stuff).

167

THE SMART GIRL'S GUIDE TO **YOUR DREAM JOB**

For wannabe photographers, it's a little easier to find success as there are loads of opportunities in areas including advertising, fashion and editorial photography, commercial and industrial photography, medical photography . . . and more! The first step is to decide which specialisation interests you most. But be warned – some areas, like advertising, fashion and editorial photography are very popular. Applicants will need loads of determination to succeed – but if you're prepared to start at the bottom, you could eventually find yourself at the top!

Contacts
Art & Design On Line
Design Edge Ltd, 7 Thistletown House, 45 Earlsfield Road,
 London SW18 3DB
Tel: 020 8265 5432
E-mail: admin@design-edge.co.uk   Website: www.design-edge.co.uk

Association of Photographers
81 Leonard Street, London EC2A 4QS
Tel: 020 7739 6669
E-mail: aop@dircon.co.uk   Website: www.aophoto.co.uk

British Institute of Professional Photography

2 Amwell End, Ware, Hertfordshire SG12 9HN

Tel: 01920 464011

E-mail: bipp@compuserve.com   Website: www.bipp.com

MUSICIAN

If you play the guitar better than Fran from Travis, or your keyboard skills could put Taylor Hanson to shame, maybe a fantastic future as a musician is ahead of you.

Professional musicians tend to work as soloists as well as in orchestras, in bands, or even as 'session' musicians (hey, you might suddenly be booked to play your cello on the new Britney single!).

Most have training to degree level (this isn't so true for the pop stars, but then they're not really famous for playing their instruments, are they?!). To get on a degree course at music college, you should have reached an advanced level (at least grade eight) before you leave school. Academically, five GCSEs and an A level or two, probably including music, will be required.

But it's not enough to simply be good at what you do. You must also love music, and have great stamina, determination and people skills.

Many musicians will teach to supplement their income, others take this up as a career in itself.

Contacts

Incorporated Society of Musicians

10 Stratford Place, London W1C 1AA

Tel: 020 7629 4413

E-mail: membership@ism.org   Website: www.ism.org

METIER (The national training organisation for the arts and entertainment industries)

Glyde House, Glydegate, Bradford, West Yorkshire BD5 0BQ

Tel: 01274 738800

E-mail: admin@metier.org.uk   Website: www.metier.org.uk

British Phonographic Industry (see their Music Education Directory)

25 Saville Row, London W1S QES

Tel: 020 7287 4422

Website: www.bpi.co.uk

DJ

Your mum might think a DJ is something your dad

wears to a posh dinner, but most of us know that there are three main types out there. And none of them wears a bow tie and wing collar shirt.

Radio DJ: People like Sara Cox, Scott Mills, Dr Fox or Margharita Taylor present shows on the radio, playing records but also introducing them, interviewing guests and generally chit-chatting about nothing. Many of these people started out on hospital or community radio, before getting their own shows on professional stations. Scott Mills, for example, had his own breakfast show in Hampshire when he was just 16!

Club DJ: Sonique, Pete Tong and Judge Jules are all club DJs, renowned for their skill in mixing different records on decks, and getting crowds of sweaty people to 'large it' on a Saturday night. Many start at private parties or community events. Nowadays, it's possible to go on courses, but nothing can make up for practising in your bedroom.

Mobile DJ: Look, it's not even worth going there. Who wants to be stuck playing old Phil Collins tunes at weddings when you're 50?

Contacts
The Radio Authority
Holbrook House, 14 Great Queen Street, London WC2B 5DG
Tel: 020 7430 2724

BBC Radio 1
Yalding House, 152 Great Portland Street, London W1N 6AJ
Tel: 020 7580 4468
Website: www.bbc.co.uk/radio1

95.8 Capital FM
30 Leicester Square, London WC2H 7LA
Tel: 020 7766 6000
Website: www.capitalfm.com

The Radio and TV School of Excellence
7–9 The Broadway, Newbury, Berkshire RG14 1AS
Tel: 01635 232800
E-mail: lisa@bbme.co.uk   Website: www.radiotvschool.co.uk

PROFESSIONAL SPORTSWOMAN

It takes someone with outstanding talent, dedica-
tion and perseverance to get as far as Anna
Kournikova, Venus Williams, Michael Owen or

Laura Davis. Most professional sportspeople will have started as brilliant amateurs at school, town or county level and if this is you, then there's hope!

There are opportunities for women in all kinds of sports, from golf to tennis and showjumping to athletics. Even football is becoming more accessible, with Fulham Football Club recently creating the first professional women's team in the UK. Contact the governing body for your sport for further details about what to do next. Be warned – you'll have a short shelf-life, but there are plenty of opportunities for you elsewhere in the field after you retire.

Even if this isn't for you, there are many thousands of unsung heroes in sport, who work in areas like coaching, leisure management, sports science and physiotherapy.

Contacts

Sport England

16 Upper Woburn Place, London WC1H 0QP

Tel: 020 7273 1500

E-mail: info@english.sports.gov.uk   Website: www.english.sports.gov.uk

Sport Scotland

Caledonia House, Southgile, Edinburgh EH12 9DQ

Tel: 0131 317 7200

Website: www.sportscotland.org.uk

Sports Council for Northern Ireland

Upper Malone Road, Belfast BT9 SLA

Tel: 028 9038 1222

Website: www.sportni.org

Sports Council for Wales

Ty-r-Gindod, Heol Allt-y-Cnap, Johntown, Carmarthen SA31 3NE

Tel: 01267 233924

Website: www.sports-council-wales.co.uk

National Council for Sport, Recreation and Allied Occupations (SPRITO)

24–32 Stephenson Way, London NW1 2HD

Tel: 020 7388 7755

E-mail: the.nto@sprito.org.uk   Website: www.sprito.org.uk

Women's Sport Foundation

305–315 Hither Green Lane, London SE13 6TJ

Tel: 020 8697 5370

National Coaching Foundation
114 Cardigan Road, Headingley, Leeds LS6 3BJ
Tel: 0113 274 4802
E-mail: coaching@ncf.org.uk   Website: www.ncf.org.uk

Institute of Leisure and Amenity Management
ILAM House, Lower Basildon, Reading, Berkshire RG8 9NE
Tel: 01491 874800
E-mail: info@ilam.co.uk   Website: www.ilam.co.uk

British Federation of Sport and Exercise Sciences (BASES)
114 Cardigan Road, Headingley, Leeds LS6 3BJ
Tel: 0113 289 1020
Website: www.bases.co.uk

Chapter 23

CVs & INTERVIEWS

Some pop stars or models have never prepared a *curriculum vitae* (CV), but they're in the minority. In fact, nearly everyone's got one, as this important piece of paper tells a future employer all about them.

And it's certain that everyone will have had an interview of some sort – whether that's an informal chat lasting just five minutes, or a series of grillings in front of a panel of five people!

So now you've decided on your dream job, how do you write a CV to guarantee you an interview? And what on earth do you say to the interviewer when you're a bundle of nerves? Here's where you find out . . .

CVs Made Easy

So you've finally reached the day when you want to apply for a job.

Wanted! Bright young spark to work for the company of your dreams, in the job you've always wanted! the ad might read (well, something like that).

Fine, you think. That's mine! But then you see the small print: *Send your CV and a covering letter to . . .*

Don't panic! Your CV isn't something to be frightened of – it's a powerful tool to help convince people you're right for the job. Even so, it's amazing how many people have CVs that look or sound bad, or undersell them.

By following the checklist below, you should be able to produce a CV that works for you and avoids all the common pitfalls.

CV checklist

Always wordprocess your CV, and send print-outs rather than photocopies. Use plain, white A4

177

paper. It might be tempting to use fluorescent orange, but most employers will hate it. Make use of bold, italic or underlining, but don't overdo it. And stick to one font!

Don't write a novel or come over all emotional – keep it short and to the point on a maximum of two sides of A4, but probably one side when you're starting out. And get at least two people to check it for any errors. Remember that typing mistakes are not always picked up by a spell checker!

Make sure you include the following details, in this order:

1 Your personal details — name, address, phone number, age/date of birth, status (not essential).

2 Your education and qualifications, starting with the most recent first.

3 Employment history – anything relevant at this stage, with most recent employment listed first. Include dates, name of the company, your job title, and give a short description of what you did. If you're applying to be a chef, it would help to say you've worked holidays in a local restuarant. It won't help to say you delivered the local free paper when you were 11.

4 Any additional information. Are you a member of a relevant club? Can you play an instrument? This helps show what kind of person you are. Information about additional skills – e.g. whether you can drive or if you have software skills, like Microsoft Word, can also help.

5 References — two people, sometimes one professional and one personal, sometimes both professional, who can vouch for your skills, ability and character.

Your covering letter

Whenever you send a CV, it should be accompanied by a covering letter. This should be short and to the point – it's your CV that's going to sell you, and you can explain more about your rare butterfly collection if you're asked about it at the interview, without including all this irrelevant detail in a covering letter.

Like your CV, keep it on white A4 paper – preferably wordprocessed.

Make sure you mention:

• Reference to the advertisement where you saw the job.

- Reference to your enclosed CV without repeating it.
- Any additional points you briefly wish to make – maybe just a couple of sentences about why you'd like the job and what you have to offer the company you're applying to.

Do not include:
- Anything too personal.
- A repeat of everything on your CV.
- Any references like "I look forward to hearing from you/seeing you at interview." This presumes far too much!

Interviews

So your CV has done its job and sold you enough to get you an interview for the job of your dreams. Well done!

But you're only halfway there. Now comes the interview – the real test, and another chance to sell yourself to the full.

What will make you better than everyone else? Well, although no two interviews are the same, doing or thinking about the following will help:

- Do some research into the company. How big is it? How long has it been going? How many other people do the job you're applying for? Is there a website you can look at? Can you ring a junior member of the company and pick their brains?
- Find out as much as you can about the industry. If it's your dream job, chances are you'll already know more about it than you think!
- Prepare answers to the common questions you'll get asked, like these and others:
  What makes this company different from its competitors?
  Why do you want to work here?
  What can you offer the company?
  What are your strengths . . . and weaknesses?
  Where do you see yourself in five years' time? (People often say they want the interviewer's job. DON'T!)
- Arrive on time, dressed appropriately.
- Don't be afraid to ask questions yourself!
- Above all, don't panic – the interviewer's likely to be as nervous as you!

Thoughts of the Future

While you're thinking about your future, here are some "Final Thoughts", Jerry Springer style!

- Chosen the wrong course at uni? Well, it's never too late to switch – talk to your advisor.

- Want somewhere else to look for jobs? In a recent survey, nearly two thirds of empolyees had found their job through networking – talking to people already in the industry.

- Not getting a response to your CV? Don't bombard people with it – you might as well be dropping hundreds from a plane at 35,000 feet! Identify the companies which might employ you, then target them with a specific letter.

- Rejected at interview stage? Go back over your CV and check there are no problems. Then ask yourself if the jobs you've applied for really suit you. Remember you can also ask for feedback on interviews!

- Want to set up your own company? Working for yourself can be a great idea, but it's not easy – get advice first.

- Not enjoying work? The people you work with make a lot of difference. And the same job can be very different in different companies. Just because you have a bad experience with one employer, it probably won't be the same elsewhere!

Chapter 24

TAKING IT FURTHER

Every one of the chapters in Section Two is stuffed
with useful phone numbers and addresses (postal,
e-mail and website) where you can find further
information about your dream job.

But what if you just want some general careers
advice? Or what if the mainstream careers are as
appealing as Marilyn Manson's sweaty socks? Say
you'd like to become a hypnotist, demolition con-
tractor, or even an ice-cream flavour developer? Or
what about a window dresser, a pilot, a driving
instructor, or a health and safety officer? You could
even be a recruitment consultant – helping other
people find their dream jobs! What we're trying to

say is that there are thousands of different careers out there which can't be squeezed into this book — otherwise it would put *War And Peace* to shame! So, if you'd like to think a bit more about the options open to you, this is your chapter.

These websites and phone lines can give you information about jobs you never dreamed even existed. Then they'll give you the lowdown on the day-to-day — from the work involved to the pay you'll take home.

Take Some Advice
InfoYouth
Website: www.infoyouth.com
Advice by young people, for young people, from higher education decisions to going into employment for the first time.

It's Your Choice 2000
Website: www.dfee.gov.uk/iyc.htm
Advice on education and training courses at 16.

Reed
Website: www.reed.co.uk
Cool careers advice, plus loads of jobs, too. Even link up to careers sites from around the world!

London Univeristy Careers Site

Website: www.careers.lon.ac.uk

Heaps of advice on applying for jobs, handling interviews, and news of holiday work and upcoming careers fairs. There's loads here!

Careers Library

You'll find the address of your local careers library in the phone book.

Careers Portal

Website: www.careers-portal.co.uk

A directory and search engine for careers info.

Reach For The Sky

Website: www.sky.com/rfts

Yet more careers advice for teens.

Universities and Colleges Admission Service

Website: www.ucas.ac.uk

Tips on filling in your uni or college application form, and much more.

Just The Job

Website: www.bbc.co.uk/wales/justthejob

BBC-produced careers advice site.

Find Me a Job!

Prospects

Website: www.prospects.csu.ac.uk

A website for graduates, with job listings, advice on filling in application forms, and 'Prospects Direct' which will search for your dream job, and e-mail you when it comes up!

Employment Service Direct

Tel: 0845 6060234

A job centre on the phone! Tell them about your qualifications, and they'll go through all full and part-time vacancies.

Job Hunter

Website: www.jobhunter.co.uk

Thousands of jobs from local newspapers around the UK, updated daily. Can select by your dream job, or by where you want to work!

Monster

Website: www.monster.co.uk

Fill in the on-line CV and this large job site will magically find you suitable vacancies. Includes great advice on writing your CV.

Careers Service

Website: www.prospects.csu.man.ac.uk

News of recruitment fairs for graduates.

Top Jobs

Website: www.topjobs.co.uk

Careers advice and links to loads of recruitment agencies and professional organisations.

Job Centre

You'll find the number for your local job centre, where hundreds of full- and part-time jobs are advertised, in the phone book.

Going It Alone

Business Link

Tel: 0345 567765

Can provide details of your local Business Link, a one-stop shop for local business advice and support.

Training and Enterprise Councils

Website: www.tec.co.uk

For advice on apprenticeships and national traineeships, as well as information on setting up your own business.

The Prince's Trust

Tel: 0800 842842

Website: www.princes-trust.org.uk

Helps 14–30-year-olds to develop confidence, learn new skills and get into work.

Livewire

Hawthorn House, Forth Banks, Newcastle-upon-Tyne NE1 3SG

Tel: 0191 261 5584

Provides information on starting your own business.

Chambers of Commerce

Once you become a member (you've set up your own business!), they'll provide guidance. Call your local branch (in the phone book) for details.

So there you have it, a giant leap towards your dream job . . . sorted!

But if you ever get stuck again, just do this: think about what you enjoy and how you would enjoy working (alone or with people? In a suit or jeans and trainers?). Then decide where you want to live, how much time you want to dedicate to work and how much flexibility you'd like.

But above all, think about what you will find interesting and fun, and give it a go. Your dream job will be exciting, fulfilling and rewarding . . . if you make it that way!

INDEX

If you would like more information about books available from Piccadilly Press and how to order them, please contact us at:

Piccadilly Press Ltd.
5 Castle Road
London
NW1 8PR

Tel: 020 7267 4492
Fax: 020 7267 4493

www.piccadillypress.co.uk